DECOMPOSING MODERNITY

DECOMPOSING MODERNITY

Ernest Becker's Images of Humanity at the End of an Age

Stephen W. Martin

Institute for Christian Studies
and
University Press of America, Inc.
Lanham • New York • London

Copyright © 1997 by
University Press of America,® Inc.
4720 Boston Way
Lanham, Maryland 20706

3 Henrietta Street
London, WC2E 8LU England

Library of Congress Cataloging-in-Publication Data

Martin, Stephen W.
Decomposing modernity : Ernest Becker's images of humanity at the
end of an age / Stephen W. Martin
p. cm.
Includes bibliographical references and Index.
l. Man. 2. Civilization, Modern--1950- 3. Becker, Ernest. I. Title
BD450.M2772 1996   128--dc20   96-38529 CIP

ISBN 0-7618-0536-2 (cloth: alk. ppr.)
ISBN 0-7618-0537-0 (pbk: alk. ppr.)

♾™ The paper used in this publication meets the minimum
requirements of American National Standard for information
Sciences—Permanence of Paper for Printed Library Materials,
ANSI Z39.48—1984

Contents

Preface

I am assured by colleagues who are experienced in such matters that a certain amount of trepidation accompanying submission of a work to a publisher is not unusual. Hence I feel my reactions to the impending publication of this work to be quite normal. Nonetheless it has been difficult to place this work into the public domain, and a few words of autobiography might help set its more personal context.

This essay is the result of a year of intense and personal struggle to come to terms with what a contemporary proponent of Enlightenment ideas concluded was the dark side of human existence. (As my then housemates could testify, living Becker's dream by proxy during that year did not make me the most cheerful of persons to live with!)

Like many of my generation, I grew up with the vision of an ever-improving world, the notion that science and the march of ideas would inevitably bring human liberation—if only we could refrain from destroying ourselves. I became a Christian in 1978 and embraced a world-denying Christianity where the world was associated with modernity. I took refuge in denying its pain by referring protest to a vague "beyond." This Christianity, almost pre-modern in its naiveté, nevertheless tacitly supported its more violent face, as the Reagan years demonstrated rather conclusively.

Convinced that the power of Christianity could not be reduced to its more conservative manifestations, I began a quest for a more *transforming* Christianity that took the world and its brokenness seriously as locus for Christian discipleship, which engaged the malformed world of modernity at its religious core and which looked to a world transformed into the kingdom of God. This work represents a crucial crossing point in this journey between these worlds.

Is this work, then, conceived in personal struggle, of public interest? I remain convinced it is. The uncritical spirit that seems to underlie recent publications from North America about the future makes me realize all the more that the West has yet to confront with honesty and integrity its ambiguous heritage. Nostalgia for that dream that moved Ernest Becker to write in the Sixties and early Seventies remains. As long as the Carl Sagans of the world continue to display a blindness to the "demons" that have "haunted" the scientific enterprise since the Enlightenment, its call needs to sound out.

I am only too aware that this work comes out of a North American, western context, a context where deconstruction predominates the cultural and academic ethos. Since 1993 I have lived and worked in South Africa, where the machinery of apartheid has been dismantled and where reconstruction is in the air. I left a Canada where the very idea of a nation was held in great scepticism. I came to a country where nation-building is an active goal mobilizing people to embrace a new future as its own—not simply as a mere outpost of Europe. And yet, as I write, the radio is broadcasting the hearings of South Africa's Truth and Reconciliation Commission, and the horrors and atrocities committed by the defenders of European "civilization" make it plain that modernity in its colonial thrust still has a lot to answer for. If this ambitious Truth Commission has one lesson for those of us in the West, it is that the way to the future is in facing the horror of the past, then letting it go on order to embrace a new life.

It is customary (again I am told) to acknowledge those who have contributed, directly or indirectly, to the production of a work. Let it be said that as much as this work is an expression of a personal struggle in a wider cultural context, it was also produced within a community of faith-ful scholarship: the Institute for Christian Studies in Toronto. But four persons especially deserve mention. I may have had many supervisors in the course of my career, but I will only have one "mentor." James Olthuis's presence-with me and his encouragement to face the darkness empowered the completion of the work and continues to inspire me. Brian Walsh, Richard Middleton and Nik Ansell offered friendship and invaluable scholarly advice at a variety of cafes along Bloor Street—always stimulating, in more ways than one! Through all these persons I have learned that scholarship at its best touches and affirms life. If this work and its dark subject touches life, or points the way, it owes that to the influence of Jim, Brian, Richard and Nik. Professor Donald Evans of the University of Toronto was kind enough to act as outside examiner for this work in its first phase, and I acknowledge his encouragement. Sally Kenel has offered valuable advice. Bob VanderVennen has shepherded this work through its second phase, and has displayed great patience in seeing it to this point. None of the aforementioned should be blamed if this work fails to fulfil its promises, academic or otherwise.

Finally, this work is dedicated to the memory of my father, William Martin. His courage and example in the face of suffering and death continue with me. Not only this, but it drastically relativizes anything I could ever read or write about the topic of death.

Cape Town, South Africa
Easter, 1996

Introduction

An autumnal chill is in the air; its similarity to the chill in other periods of cultural decline is undeniable. One can point not only to vast shifts in geopolitical balances of power but also to the apparent disintegration of our reigning ideologies (East and West alike). It is even more the sense ... that the intellectual and spiritual heart of the culture, its confidence in science, technology and an expanding industrialism, has come upon difficult if not self contradictory and self destructive days, and that the culture as a whole is thus entering a "time of troubles" of very deep scope.

Langdon Gilkey[1]

The harvest is past, the summer is ended, and we are not saved.

Jeremiah 8:20[2]

The "Fall" of Modernity

In the space of a few months the world as westerners knew it came to an end. Those events, centred around the advent season of 1989, overtook with a blinding speed. The Berlin Wall fell, the Iron Curtain lifted from Eastern Europe (ending the forty year long "cold war"—and the just cause for those on the right) and Nelson Mandela was released from prison while F.W. de Klerk (whose power embodied perhaps the most popular "cause" on the left) promised reform. The old enemies disappeared and a "new world order" was inaugurated.

At least that was the view from Washington. It seemed fitting that Francis Fukuyama had in the summer of that year proclaimed "the end of history." The grand dream of modernity, its progress myth, seemed to have been fulfilled in the events of that year. Like in the ending of a western, "the good guys had won." But there was little or no celebration. For a deeper malaise remained in the hearts, if not the heads, of western people.

Take for example the recession that the world plunged into shortly after these events; or take the environmental disasters, (most notably in 1989 that of the *Exxon Valdez*), poisoning sea and sky to feed the mechanisms of modernity;[3] or take the petty little war that started against Iraq under the pretences of the "new world order," a war which pommelled a country for the sake of liberating a repressive dictatorship; or take simply the fact that the triumph of capitalism over communism has quietly repressed the reality that economic inequality grows in the free market west. "The capitalist economies are producing nations of financiers who live in mansions and hamburger flippers who can't afford an apartment."[4] Bob Goudzwaard uses the image of "cumulation and frustration" in describing the way modernity's problems are mounting on top of each other.[5]

Besides these environmental, economic and military problems, there is the resurgence of "identity politics," especially in those parts of the world previously held together within the tension of cold war. Ethnic cleansing in the former Yugoslavia and uprisings in the former Soviet Union threaten to extend the aftershocks of 1989 into the dawn of the new millennium. While all this is going on fundamentalism and neoconservatism, the American (and Canadian) version of ethnic, religious and class idolatries, tightens its xenophobic grip over people's sensibilities.

Reading such seismic occurrences as heralding what pop group REM calls "the end of the world as we know it," sensitive cultural observers are concluding that we live in a declining age where the ground continually gives way under old certainties. This is not a new theme. In the early sixties Bob Dylan wrote of an "old order rapidly aging," but also of a "new one" on the horizon. What is different thirty years later is that there is no certainty about what new thing is coming, and that the belief that the new is necessarily better has eroded with the loss of belief in inevitable progress. As we approach the end of the millennium, and as the circles of poverty and affluence, of war and peace wind tighter, the apocalyptic spirit gripping the west grows more intense. Bookstores are filled with titles with "ending" and "beyond" words. "Things are going to slide in all directions," prophesies Leonard Cohen in his song, "The Future," "Won't be nothing you can measure any more." Even those who can profess to have "seen the future" conclude "It is murder."[6]

Where Enlightenment optimism sung a secularized version of *Amazing Grace* ("I once was lost but now am found, was blind but now I see."), now theologian Douglas John Hall uses the metaphor of "night" to describe the modern sense.[7] Once Enlightenment denoted "the dawning of a new day." Now Langdon Gilkey talks about an "autumnal chill" and Robert Heilbroner about the end of "prome-thean man"[8] in its wake. But not all are as negative as these three. Walter Truett Anderson, for instance, talks of a new "postmodern" consciousness arising out of the fragmented horizons of modernity.[9] And Ernest Becker, the subject of the present work, thought that a time of death was also potentially a time of rebirth; that a time of decline was also potentially a time of renewal.[10]

Is there a connection between these general, yet deeply felt, events and trends in the west? Are these symptoms of a deeper "Malaise of Modernity"?[11] An insightful diagnosis of our times is desperately needed, one that looks behind the headlines and underneath the appearances (symptoms) to address the driving motives of a culture, its impelling spirit. At the same time it must be sensitive to those artifacts (symbols, stories, songs) which identify the culture, where its spirit is incarnate. Such a reading dares, as Goudzwaard says, to hold up a mirror and to look ourselves full in the face.[12] This is a hard thing to do, however, since in questioning our tradition we also question ourselves. It is a sign of the times that what David Tracy has called the "plurality and ambiguity" of all traditions[13] is now gradually being acknowledged. And it is a sign of the times that *our* tradition—the very one that called into question all "other" traditions—has become questionable. Was the Enlightenment aptly named as the coming of age of humanity, or is Alasdair MacIntyre right when he says that it was a period of deepest darkness, where humanity actually lost its way?

Self-examination is the watchword for some. And in modernity's dark night of the soul, its "time of trials" (as Langdon Gilkey called it in the introductory quotation), the questionability of the modern project brings "the gravest sort of anxiety."[14] If Lesslie Newbigin is right in saying that "Enlightenment" is a conversion word[15] then this anxiety concerns modernity's deepest religious roots.

It is therefore urgent that, at the end (in both the temporal and existential sense of "ending") of the twentieth century, modernity confront its own self-images. This means recalling the hopes which gave birth to the modern spirit, as well as the fears which now characterize its demise.

A number of important studies of the crisis of modernity have been written in the past five years, including some from a Christian point of view.[16] This present study is not simply an attempt to come to terms with the modernity/postmodernity issue; this would be to repeat what has been said elsewhere. It is rather more like a case study built around the journey of a particular modern person whose writings exemplify the dream and the dread of modernity.

Ernest Becker: The Dream of (an) Enlightenment Man

Becker's Images of Human Existence

In the writings of Ernest Becker (1924-1974), the highs and the lows, the hopes and the fears, the anticipation and the dread that seem to characterize the modern spirit are particularly evident. That is why he is the object of this study. Becker—who was described by a former student as "a man who exemplified, in both his teaching and scholarship, a passionate and profound commitment to humanist values"[17]— once shared in that Enlightenment faith that saw the earth as a stage for the future apotheosis of humanity. He claimed that this faith needed to spread into the present time, that humans needed to uncover their own potential as autonomous creatures. And yet Becker also came to see that autonomy was an illusion, and that humanity's career on the planet was incidental to the earth.[18]

Becker once identified the human person as "the animal that holds up a mirror to himself."[19] When he looked into the mirror, Becker saw two images reflecting back. He termed these images *homo poeta* and *homo heroica*. The former saw humanity as a product of a grand process of emergent evolution, the pinnacle of nature striving toward freedom. This vision is characterized by optimism concerning human possibility. If humans could but complete the process of detachment from instinctive behaviour, from following "the herd," from the constraints of "culture," then the fulfilment of the life process would be achieved.

But this image was too optimistic. Later Becker came to see that it screened out too easily the vicious behaviour that humanity was capable of, and that modern humanity was indeed doing. Coming to terms with the dark side meant for Becker formulating a new image. *Homo heroica* reflects an ontological paradox. Limitless horizons are now limited by nature, particularly by the body. The attempt to formulate a limitless horizon is done in the teeth of nature, and is the origin of humanly created evil. Autonomy is an illusion. Humanity must now adapt and wait.

While different in these ways, both these images are animated by the same spirit: a modern spirit that identified humanity as the open creature and the earth as meaningful only in terms of being a "stage" for its emergence. And now to the thrust of this work.

Facing the Death of Modernity's Self-Images

Ernest Becker's most famous work, entitled *The Denial of Death*, contended that humanity is located in the interstices of paradox, that humanity's quest for a world as stage for transcendence in spite of limitations forms the basic context for all human activity. He claimed that death is a complex symbol that speaks not simply of decay into the grave, but of the loss of control over self and world. Since this is precisely the way that many contemporary people experience their world, this work explores the writings of Becker as a tracing out of this awareness as that of a modern person facing a world well lost. It especially takes note of the sense of homelessness in the world disclosed by both images. These images, and their death, must be "owned" and "let go" before newness can be hoped for. Ernest Becker can help show us the way to new trust and hope.

The remainder of this introduction is concerned with context. The first is the context of Becker's own work: How was it received? The second sets the context of the present work: How does it build upon and differ from other studies of Becker? The third concerns the broader societal context: what are some of the salient features of modernity relevant to a study of Becker?

The two chapters exegete the two images of human existence presented by Becker. Chapter one begins with an examination of Becker's early ontology wherein the striving life process is seen as oriented toward freedom, which means freedom from enslavement to pre-programmed instincts. It shall present Becker's view of humanity as the open creature, boundless in horizon, potentially creating its own world—and recreating itself—in rendering a grey and neutral world meaningful. Becker's understanding of culture as the way this process was compromised by an enslavement to the will of the herd which he termed "symbolic reinstinctivization" will be illumined. The chapter closes by examining Becker's claim that criticism of the self and of culture opened the way to authentic individuality.

The second chapter starts with Becker's own self-criticism of his suppression of the dark side of human striving. The way he characterised *homo heroica* as working a distinctive gift onto the world considered no longer as grey and neutral but as violent and irrational will come under scrutiny. The creature, formerly imagined with limitless horizons, is now reimagined as radically limited, as finite and mortal, fraught with ontological paradoxes. Becker's criticism of those (including himself in his earlier writings) who saw human nature as transformable is highlighted. It is in paradox rather than possibility that human nature is located, and without paradox human nature would be impossible. We must balance the tensions between individuation and identification and between narcissistic self-inflation and yielding to others. The way to do this, Becker concludes, is to reassert religion.

These two chapters are followed by a brief resume which examines continuities and discontinuities within these images. Both images display the view that meaning is found in autonomous control and that the fall of humanity consists in the loss of control. Discontinuity is displayed in the contrast between *homo poeta* who loses control in a process of socialization (and who therefore can regain it by overcoming society) and *homo heroica* in whom the loss of control is constitutive to its being. The conclusion is entitled "A World Well Lost" because, out of control, modern humanity loses the world in trying to gain itself and tragically winds up losing itself as well.

It follows that modern humanity must face its own end and hope for resurrection. Therefore this work concludes with the image of a requiem vigil. Here the key is that "humanity" and "modern humanity" are not coterminus (something moderns have had trouble with). To return to the mirror image, Becker has shown us what we as moderns are. Only in facing it can we hope beyond its demise.

Approaching Ernest Becker

Becker and the Social Sciences

Throughout his career Becker was a marginal figure in his own area of academic interest. Becker's writings, especially his earlier ones, received mixed reviews in the world of academic social science. While Philip Bosserman thought that Becker's work "could not be more timely," and that *The Structure of Evil* "could very well have been the basic source for the Stockholm Conference" (in 1969 on "The Place of Value in a World of Fact"),[20] others were not nearly as kind.[21]

Robert Jay Lifton noted in his review of *Escape From Evil*, that Becker had a reputation of being, "wildly associative, dramatically existential ... and less than systematic."[22] Consequently his ideas have not been developed to any large extent. There is no "Becker School of Thought" to which we can appeal. There are no *festschriften* giving variations on his themes.[23] There are no disciples carrying on his legacy.[24] Recovering the significance of Becker for today necessitates turning elsewhere.

Becker and Theology

The fact that his writings never received wide acceptance in the social sciences never seemed to bother Becker. Right before he died Becker said that his greatest contribution was actually in the delivering over of the social sciences to a merger with theology.[25] Indeed some theologians have made use of Becker's writings. Douglas John Hall and Sally Kenel, for example, use Becker as a dialogue partner for developing "contextual" and "fundamental" theologies respectively. Their work is aimed at the construction of a "relevant" theology which appeals to the "mainstream" academy.[26]

Hall, for example, sees much potential in Becker's idea of the "creative illusion" as pointing to the reappearance of religion in relation to the darkness of our time. Becker's work focusing on the dark side of human existence opens up space for a theology of the cross—a strong motive in Hall's own theological program. While insightful in some ways, Hall's reading of Becker fails in its affirmation of Becker's problematic view of the nature of truth and its relation to repression. Becker's claim that we need "creative illusions" is founded, as shall be demonstrated in chapter two, on the Enlightenment distinction between "truth," "reality," and "science" on the one hand and "meaning," "myth" and "religion" on the other. Hall's work, while attempting to "lighten our darkness" through Becker's "vision in the night" winds up simply holding forth modernity's flickering candle.[27]

Like most treatments of Becker, Hall and Kenel also tend to pick and choose among Becker's works, especially concentrating on *The Denial of Death*. While their expositions are generous, they bracket off Becker's earlier work, which in its optimism sets up his later view of humanity as a tragic figure. It is the contention of the present work that Becker's later writings can only be adequately understood when read in the light of his earlier work.[28]

One exception to this bracketing tendency might be Frederick Sontag. In his collection of essays entitled *The Return of the Gods*,[29] Sontag does focus his attention on Becker's earlier work. However, Sontag fails to recognize any development in Becker's writings, attacking him as a static entity. He employs Becker as proof text in supporting his agenda of recovering theology and metaphysics as classical disciplines contemporary thinkers have "lost" and need to regain. Sontag is simply wrong when he claims that Becker tries, unsuccessfully, to do away with the gods. "Proving" his point that we need to get back to "old fashioned theology" involves making Becker a scapegoat.

Other theologians have treated Becker's concepts to a careful scrutiny, chiefly concerning the way Becker uses terms like "finitude" and "transcendence" to illuminate human existence.[30] Unfortunately, Becker's synthetic style and underlying integrative intentions make such an approach difficult. He himself admitted that he sacrificed theoretical precision for the sake of communicating his urgent message.[31]

Indeed Becker has been criticized for this loose use of concepts.[32] However when one recognizes Becker as trying to accommodate an entire tradition, that of Enlightenment social science, and to integrate it into a framework that reveals what he thought was its transforming power, it is understandable why his terms are so often amorphous.[33] If "the human sciences" have revealed what and who we really are, then the contributions of each science[34] are valid to this larger understanding. Like stained glass, each colours in its own way the light that shines on the human condition from the Enlightenment. It is "the larger understanding" that this work is interested in. It explores Becker's conceptual apparatus only in order to answer the question: What does Becker see when he looks at human activity through the human sciences?

The present work is interested in vision. *Modern* vision. It tries to look, *with* Becker, into the mirror images of modernity. Its guiding assumption will be that what someone sees, especially a sensitive observer like Becker, is related to a fundamental vision of humanness. This vision is dynamic, not static. It is formulated continually in interaction with the newspapers, journal articles, relationships and setbacks that make up one's life in culture.

This fundamental vision then, identified in Becker as being both optimistic and tragic, is the focus of this work. Fundamental visions are not simply aesthetic in character, however. The qualifier "fundamental" means that such visions concern the very ground of one's existence, an accounting for evil and hope for redemption. That is, they are faith visions involving fundamental trust.

The language of "trust" is the language of theology. Therefore it may be said that this work is *theological*. But faith visions are also *communal*. They are, as we indicated above, incarnated in the *cultural* life of a people. Hence the particular kind of study undertaken here—its special angle of approach to Becker—may be stated as *theology of culture*.[35]

Since this is specifically a theology of *modern* culture, one more step must be taken before encountering Ernest Becker. Before proceeding to his two different pictures, a frame must be constructed. Some of the salient features of modernity relevant to this study will now be highlighted.[36]

The Culture of Modernity

From Dark Ages to Enlightenment

The use of the term "modern" creates a difficulty of definition. "Modern" is commonly used in the sense of the "developed" third of the world (e.g., "modern" vs. "pre-modern" societies). "Modern" is also used as the cumulation of the historical process, as the highest "level" of civilization (e.g., "modernization"). Sometimes modern simply means "contemporary" (as in "modern music").

In the psyches of "modern" people, there is a shared conviction that the one third of the world dominated by European males is the highest cultural realization of human dominion over nature.[37] Generally speaking, this "culture of modernity" is said to have been birthed in the decline of the Middle Ages. While modern people speak of this predecessor period as "the Dark Ages" (and hence the "Enlightenment" as its successor), it is important (and ironic) to note that the groping for meaning is a feature of modernity. Why this is so will become apparent below.

Nevertheless, "modern" usually means "advanced." Part of what constituted "advancement" for Becker was modern humanity's self-awareness of the contingent, constructed nature of all social structures.[38] "In the perspective of history, it seems inevitable that man should have ended up by 'seeing through himself,' as it were."[39]

The metaphor of "seeing through" is telling. Perhaps the term that defines the modern age best is "criticism." The Enlightenment, so Becker thought, relentlessly subjected all human phenomena to criticism. No longer accepting any particular social system, type of government or way of constructing the world as "the true one," moderns like Becker view humanity, more than anything else, as a "world maker" rather than simply as "world dweller." Perhaps even more radically, however, was the idea correlative with the criticism of myths of timeless social order: that humanity could also be a world "unmaker."

The ability to take note of the way societies were structured gives moderns what they think to be an ability to stand outside the historical process and to survey it as "leading up to" their emergence. Indeed Kant's call to modern people to "dare to know" (from his famous essay "What is Enlightenment?")[40] implied that, to that point, people had not "dared to know" but rather had taken the easy way out by believing superstitions. The difference between the Enlightenment and the pre-Enlightenment person was not of *degree but of kind*.

The Enlightenment is, for moderns, a watershed. It functions in a way similar to the Exodus in Judaism and the Crucifixion in Christianity. Indeed Becker's works continually assault the reader with statements like "today we know." "The secret is out!" says Becker the Enlightenment man. The correlative implication, at least in Becker's earlier works, is that "now that we know, we can manipulate a better world." And a better world means a better human being.[41]

Three Modern Themes

Brian Walsh and Richard Middleton characterize modernity as that venture,

> ... stretching from the Renaissance through the Enlightenment to the present day, to control nature by means of rational and technical insight and technological power for human—primarily economic—benefit. This project of control and progress, which is basic to western society, is rooted in autonomy—the secular myth that human beings are supreme in the world, that we are the self-normed masters of our own destiny, and of the destiny of the world.[42]

Three motifs of the modern spirit are present in this definition. First, modernity is rooted in a "secular myth" which displaces God in favour of humanity. Second, the thrust of modernity is "control of nature," which implies a certain vision of the way humans and non-humans interact, as well as a view of the relation between body and self. Third, the outcome of human activity is seen in "progress," the idea that the Enlightenment inaugurates a secularized utopia where "sorrow and mourning shall flee away" through human rational and technical activity. And this "utopia" is where the course of the world is heading with humanity as captain. Each of these is replicated in Becker's writings.

Secularity: The Banishment of God

"Secular" does not necessarily mean "atheistic." Bernard Zylstra is right when he says that "it is not necessary to be an atheist to be an agent of the spirit of modernity."[43] It is possible, even acceptable, for moderns to believe in God. However secularity *does* mean a certain kind of God becomes necessary to posit, if a God is to be posited at all—a God that allows, even encourages the project of human autonomy.

In this context, secularity is understand as the loss of a God actively involved in the affairs of the world. Becker saw this as a consequence of the rise of the critical human sciences which usurped Christianity in defining the world, accounting for evil and establishing norms. This is the burden of both *The Structure of Evil* and *Beyond Alienation*. And yet neither of these works make the claim that modern people should no longer believe in God.

If God may still be affirmed as "existent" in some way, the very particular revelation of God in the world claimed by any religious tradition is either done away with or generalized to the point where it becomes devoid of relevance to shared, public life. Moderns who claim to be believers in God are subject to a peculiar split between value and fact, between private and public worlds, between meaning and truth, between particularity and universality.[44] Belief in God may be acceptable as a private option for meaning, but no particular God can be accepted as universal norm for private life. As an individual I "choose" my private God, just as I choose my personal "value system."

But this supposed relegation of religion does not mean a loss of revelation *per se*. Rather the locus of revelation is changed to the sphere of human rational activity, especially the activity of science. In the modern world, science becomes the legit-imating bar of truth. For a modern to call something "scientific" is just another way of saying that it is "indisputably true."

Nature as Stage for Faustian Conquest

Coincident with this is a second feature: an idea of creation as source of revelation about humans and their ultimate point of orientation is lost. The place of humans in the world becomes a matter of "making space" rather than finding or accepting. Nature is opposed to humanity such that it must be "tamed" for human benefit; and humanity is set over against nature. Meaning is no longer seen as accepting one's place in the world as a gift. Nature has meaning inasmuch as humanity controls it through the exercise of rational powers. This is a strong theme in Becker's 1968 work *The Structure of Evil*.

Secularity and the setting of human autonomous freedom over against a nature stripped of significance connect in a view of the world as "the arena of man's

Faustian conquest."[45] But this strange term "human nature" remains. For we are, unlike the lower animals, free and yet like them we are "embodied." Becker understood this problem when he claimed that humans look up and see the stars beckoning. But they also look down and see a body which never seems to want to do what they want it to, and they look ahead and see death and decay as fate.[46]

Carrying forth the theme of the setting of autonomy over against nature means that human nature must be defined as malleable and open. While we "have" bodies, we alone can give significance to them.[47] This significance is a remaking, an attribution (or imposition) of "meaning." Putting things in this way however only underscores for modern humans what they have lost.

Progress: A Secular Utopia

The third feature is the supposed outworking of control: *progress*. Progress is the idea that as humans gain more and more control over nature (and themselves), they move closer and closer to the day when nature—and the limits of the body—are tamed and utopia is assured.[48] As Zylstra puts it, "Man's creaturely finitude is equated with his 'sinful' predicament, from which he must be liberated through self-redemption ... in order to regain paradise lost."[49] History is a staging of human apotheosis.

Becker believed that a "science of man" wherein the open and becoming nature of humanity was revealed was a key for the implementation of progress. Although this may seem to be already a relativization of the idea of inevitable progress as a law of history, he combined it with a strong faith in the supposed ability of humans to improve themselves through self-awareness, to overcome historical evil through understanding and to bring in a new world where the human spirit would be the object of worship.

No More Utopias

Bob Goudzwaard claims that it is this progress myth that embodies the dilemmas of modernity.[50] For what once seemed like an inevitable push toward secular utopia has now become a decline toward destruction. With negative progress comes loss of autonomy, of control and of a vision of "open" human nature. Moreover the world seems hostile, not amenable to human activity. The accompanying sense of disorder makes us alternate between "escapist" belief in a God that could care less about the world (as in fundamentalism) or a nihilistic renunciation of belief in God, in humanity, in anything.

Having briefly taken note of some features of modernity, the stage is set for us to approach to the images of humanity put forth by that modern man, Ernest Becker.

Notes

1. *Society and the Sacred* (New York: Crossroad, 1981), xi.

2. *Holy Bible, Revised Standard Version* (Division of Christian Education of the National Council of Churches of Christ in America, 1952).

3. Disasters had so mounted by the summer of 1989 that environmentalist David Suzuki in desperation claimed that the world had ten years to repent of its environmental sins before the damage to the earth was irreversible. "A Preview," *A Planet for the Taking*, produced by Daniel Zukerman (Toronto: CBC, 1989.)

4. See Jack Cahill, "Dark Victory: Capitalism K.O.'s Communism but not Everyone is Cheering," *Toronto Star*, Sunday, December 17, 1989: B-1.

5. *Capitalism and Progress*, translated by Josina Van Nuis Zylstra (Toronto and Grand Rapids: Wedge and Eerdmans, 1979), xiv.

6. It is not insignificant that this song was the theme of the Oliver Stone film, "Natural-Born Killers." Why this is so will become apparent in chapter two.

7. See Douglas John Hall, *Thinking the Faith* (Minneapolis: Augsburg, 1989).

8. Gilkey, *Society and the Sacred* (New York: Crossroad, 1981), xi and Robert Heilbroner, *An Inquiry into the Human Prospect*, updated and reconsidered for the 1980s (New York: Norton, 1980), 164.

9. See Walter Truett Anderson, *Reality Isn't What it Used to Be* (San Francisco: Harper-Collins, 1990).

10. "The Second Great Step in Human Evolution," *The Christian Century*, January 31, 1968: 135-37.

11. The phrase is from Charles Taylor, *The Malaise of Modernity* (Toronto: House of Anansi Press, 1992).

12. Goudzwaard is a Dutch Christian economist-philosopher. In his *Capitalism and Progress*, he claims that not only are we in the west confronted with a cluster of problems, but traditional ways of solving them are impotent and lead to even further problems. The only way through is to look deeply into the roots of western society and to discern the impelling spirit driving it. His analysis of the economic structure of the west opens up into a naming of that spirit incarnate in the structure of capitalism as "progress." This demythologization calls those very roots into question, and thus follows the mirror image.

13. *Plurality and Ambiguity* (San Francisco: Harper and Row, 1987), 8.

14. The phrase "the gravest sort of anxiety" is Clifford Geertz'. While it refers to the precariousness of all cultural constructs, it is particularly appropriate as a reading of the present crisis in modern culture. Incidently, the context from which this phrase is taken actually echoes much of what we shall hear Becker say:

> Man depends upon symbols and symbol systems with a dependence so great as to be decisive for his creatural viability and, as a result, his sensitivity to

even the remotest indication that they may prove unable to cope with one or another aspect of experience raises within him the gravest kind of anxiety.... "Religion as a Cultural System," in *The Interpretation of Cultures* (New York: Basic Books, 1973), 99.

In a chapter entitled "Modernity in Decline" in his *Langdon Gilkey: Theologian for a Culture in Decline* (Lanham, MD: University Press of America, 1991) Brian Walsh gives a litany of citations describing the present crisis in modernity. The reader who is interested in pursuing further indictments of modernity should turn there.

15. *Foolishness to the Greeks* (Grand Rapids: Eerdmans, 1986), 23.

16. From an explicitly Christian point of view see Walsh, Gilkey, Newbiggin and Goudzwaard cited above. Although he seems to wish for a return to pre-modern sensibilities, John Milbank's *Theology and Social Theory: Beyond Secular Reason* (Oxford: Blackwell, 1990) contains pertinent critiques of modernity. Two excellent introductions to postmodernity are J. Richard Middleton and Brian J. Walsh's *Truth Is Stranger Than It Used To Be* (Downers Grove: InterVarsity Press, 1995) and sociologist David Lyon's *Postmodernity* (Buckingham: Open University Press, 1994).

17. Harold Jacobs, "Ernest Becker: A Reconsideration," *Humanity and Society* 5 (1981): 239. Speaking on behalf of other students who owed a debt to Becker, Jacobs goes on to say that,

> By showing us how deeply our roots were embedded in a brilliant and humanistically-oriented historical tradition, he profoundly bolstered and sharpened our vision, previously supported only by our moral intuition, of a social science committed to maximizing human self-preservation and the unfolding of human potential (241).

18. Reading Becker's deathbed interview with Sam Keen led Harold Jacobs to remark:

> The Becker of the earlier years is almost unrecognizable. The Enlightenment vision is dwarfed by an all-pervasive sense of despair. The utopian cutting edge of his earlier social theory ... is replaced by the one-dimensional, death-bed appraisal: "I strongly suspect that it may not be possible for mankind to achieve very much on this planet." "Reconsideration": 244.

19. Sam Keen, "The Heroics of Everyday Life: A Theorist of Death Confronts His Own End," An interview with Ernest Becker, *Psychology Today* 7:11 (April 1974): 74.

20. Review of *The Structure of Evil, American Sociological Review* 35 (1970): 121.

21. An unsigned review of *The Structure of Evil* in *Choice* 5 (October, 1968): 938, called it "... a parade of Becker's personal prejudices...." and dismissed it by saying, "Not recommended unless one is collecting samples of contemporary existentialist-romantic polemic material."

22. "Further Intimations of Immortality," *New York Times Book Review*, Dec. 14, 1975: 4.

23. In the summer of 1975, *The Journal of the Otto Rank Society* (10:1, 58-80) published four commentaries on *The Denial of Death*, which it titled "Four Commentaries on an Important Book." This is the closest thing there is to a collection of essays or lectures devoted to Becker. Even these commentaries are thin and deal mainly with the question of whether Becker is or isn't a faithful interpreter of Rank.

24. Becker would have been relieved to know these things; he expressed strong disdain of "movements" and "the cult of personality." Keen, "Heroics": 80.

25. Keen, "Heroics": 71.

26. Douglas John Hall, *Thinking the Faith* (Minneapolis: Augsburg, 1989); Sally Kenel, *Mortal Gods: Ernest Becker and Fundamental Theology* (Lanham: University Press of America, 1989).

27. The same charge of evangelizing the Enlightenment in different words could be levelled against Daniel Liechty's reading of Becker in *Theology in Post-Liberal Perspective* (London: SCM Press, 1990).

28. After this work was completed in first draft, Ted Peters' book *Sin: Radical Evil in Soul and Society* (Grand Rapids: Eerdmans, 1994) appeared. Peters deals with Becker's two approaches to the problem of human evil: that of *The Structure of Evil* (1968) and *Escape from Evil* (1975), developing similar contrasts to those in the conclusion of this work. While he does not discuss them with reference to *homo poeta* and *homo heroica*, his approach has affinities with the present one.

29. Peter Lang, 1989.

30. In addition to Kenel's, two other treatments are worth mentioning: Eugene Bianchi, "Death and Transcendence in Ernest Becker," *Religion in Life* 46 (1977): 460-75, and Sebastian Moore, *The Crucified Jesus Is No Stranger* (New York: Seabury Press, 1981).

31. *Revolution*, 5-7; 36 n.1; *Structure*, 384-89.

32. Vernon K. Dibble says that

> Most works of social science, unless they are exploratory or purely descriptive ... seek to maximize (1) generality, (2) complexity, (3) precision. But as Richard Levins, the population biologist, has suggested, it is usually not possible to maximize all three values at the same time, or in the same theory, or in the same work. "Ethics, Politics and Holistic Social Science," a review essay of *The Structure of Evil* in *American Journal of Sociology* 85:5 (1980): 1236.

Dibble suggests that Becker's synthetic efforts, at least in *The Structure of Evil*, maximize generality (1234) and complexity at the expense of precision. Thus he calls Becker's theory a "discursive theory" (1236). Dibble also intimates, on 1237, that in Becker generality and complexity are in tension, which tests the applicability of Becker's theory to other spheres such as ethics. While this is a valid critique if Becker is read simply as a social scientist, the present work proposes to read him more broadly, as a cultural observer. Hence his universalistic statements are "readings" of the human condition as he envisions it.

33. Harold Jacobs, who studied under Becker, says that Becker "was a relaxed, self-assured lecturer who turned the jargon of contemporary social science into language often bordering on poetry." "Reconsideration": 242.

34. In *The Structure of Evil* Becker categorizes the human sciences as psychology (contributing a chapter on "personality and value"); social psychology (on "nature and the self"); sociology (on "the social dimensions of evil"); psychiatry (on "the law of personality development"); descriptive ontology (on "esthetics as ethics") and historical psychology (on "the union of Marx and Freud"). In *Beyond Alienation* (New York: George Braziller, 1968), he divides his disciplinary focus into a "scientific" and a "theological" dimension of a New Moral View of the World (his capitals). The scientific dimension includes psychology and sociology (together) and psychiatry. The two chapters on "the theological dimension" start with descriptive ontology and then move from there to theology. Whether theology is itself a "science" (in the same way that the others are), Becker doesn't say.

35. The term "theology of culture" was first used by Paul Tillich in his first public speech entitled *"Uber die Idee einer Theologie der Kultur."* See Tillich's collection, *Theology of Culture* (London: Oxford Press, 1959). While I acknowledge a general debt to Tillich, the two figures most influential in the present work are Langdon Gilkey and Brian Walsh. For Gilkey's definition of the term, see *Society*, ix-x. For Walsh's use of the term, and his appraisal of both Gilkey and Tillich, see *Gilkey*, 71-82.

Kelton Cobb has pointed out that Tillich's theology of culture is flawed in the way it privileges "high" over "low" culture, seeing the former as the "best" example of human creativity in a given epoch. This "Mandarin distinction between *Kultur* and *Zivilisation"* (73) is something Tillich inherited from his friends in the Frankfurt School. Following recent critics of this School, Cobb argues for culture as a human activity of shaping and forming, common to all, which discloses "a culture's deeper allegiances" (78). "Reconsidering the Status of Popular Culture in Tillich's Theology of Culture," *Journal of the American Academy of Religion* LXIII: 1, 53-84.

The disclosure of modern "deeper allegiances" and their ambiguous nature in the texts of Ernest Becker is the concern of this present work.

36. The view of modernity informing this work comes from a number of sources and the reader is referred to them for a more complete treatment. These include the works of Gilkey, Goudzwaard, Newbigin and Walsh previously cited, as well as Peter Berger, *Facing Up to Modernity* (New York: Basic Books, 1977); Charles Taylor, *Sources of the Self* (Cambridge: Harvard, 1990); Brian J. Walsh and J. Richard Middleton, *The Transforming Vision: Shaping a Christian World View* (Downers Grove: InterVarsity Press, 1984), ch. 8; Middleton and Walsh, *Truth Is Stranger Than It Used To Be: Biblical Faith in a Postmodern Age* (Downers Grove: InterVarsity Press, 1995); Bernard Zylstra, "Modernity and the American Empire," *International Reformed Bulletin* 68 (1977): 3-19; and idem, "Daniel Bell's Neo-Conservative Critique of Modernity," in *Hearing and Doing*, John Kraay and Anthony Tol, eds. (Toronto: Wedge, 1979), 15-37.

37. This is not to say that the third world (and now the second world—which is rapidly joining the third in its poverty and political upheaval) does not look to the modernized west as its model. Unfortunately it does.

38. See especially *Structure*, chapter one, and *Beyond Alienation*, passim.

39. E. Becker, *The Revolution in Psychiatry* (New York: The Free Press of Glencoe, 1964), 137.

40. Reprinted in *On History*, ed. L.W. Beck, trans. L.W. Beck, R.E. Anchor and E.L. Fackenheim (New York: Bobbs-Merrill), 1963.

41. See Milton Scarborough's *Myth and Modernity: Postcritical Reflections* (Albany: SUNY Press, 1994) for a useful treatment of the ambiguous relation between modernity and myth.

42. J. Richard Middleton and Brian J. Walsh, "Dancing in the Dragon's Jaws: Bruce Cockburn's Struggle with Modernity," *The Crucible* 2 (Spring, 1992): 11-18.

43. Bernard Zylstra, "Modernity and the American Empire," *International Reformed Bulletin* 68 (1977): 5.

44. The works of Lesslie Newbigin are most helpful in this connection. See especially *Foolishness* and *The Gospel in a Pluralistic Society* (Grand Rapids: Eerdmans, 1989). At the time of writing his most recent work was *Proper Confidence: Faith, Doubt and Certainty in Christian Discipleship* (Grand Rapids: Eerdmans, 1995). Newbigin was a missionary in India for most of his life and upon returning to his native England has wrote prolifically on the implicit dualisms within modern societies. His work is informed by Alasdair MacIntyre, whose book *After Virtue* (Notre Dame: University of Notre Dame Press, 1981) makes a similar point about the nature of "truth" in modernity.

45. Zylstra, "Modernity": 7.

46. This is a theme especially in Becker's last works, particularly *The Denial of Death*.

47. This also relates the instrumentalization of the other. The other becomes the means by which the self assures itself of its own significance. This is also a theme in

Becker in two ways. In his early work, self-esteem comes from addressing a performance to another. In his later work, the other becomes a locus of control whereby the self assures itself it is not subject to mortality.

48. See this theme especially in Goudzwaard, *Capitalism*, ch. 5.

49. Zylstra, "Modernity": 9.

50. See "The Dialectic of Progress" in *Capitalism and Progress*, 151-61.

2. Emergence and Autonomy: Homo Poeta

Fundamental Questions and the "Science of Man"

Questions about the nature and purpose of humans literally "get to the bottom" of things. Such questions,

> ... lie deep within the heart of everyone. Who am I? Where am I going? What's it all about? Is there a god? How can I live and die happily? Everyone formulates some answer to these questions about the human condition, if only partially and implicitly. The answer we give may be referred to as our world-view, or vision of life.... It makes up the framework of fundamental considerations which give context, direction and meaning to our lives.[1]

The work of Ernest Becker is best understood as a modern attempt to answer these questions. He saw his attempt as necessary, since a vision of human becoming was what the modern world lacked. His critical perspective on society claimed that since the decline of the medieval worldview, answers to such fundamental questions were profoundly lacking in depth.

Such questions (and answers) are not simply intellectual. They are answerable only by an appeal to what one considers fundamental to life. Nor are they simply matters of individual preference. They reflect a communal vision. Such questions are answered in *revelation*, in surrender to some legitimizing bar of truth. In addressing these questions, Becker invokes science, specifically "the science of man."[2] This should not be of any surprise especially in so far as Becker is a modern man and modern men (and women) appeal to science to give "the facts" about the world.[3] Such "facts" as revealed by science are set over against the fanciful myths of all predecessor cultures.

And yet Becker's view is not quite as simple as would seem. For science must be guided by a basic commitment. For Becker, this commitment is rooted in the

Enlightenment assertion: "Man is good but society renders him evil."[4] The character of the science that one develops depends on what is done with this assertion. In *Angel in Armor*, he put it this way:

> ... the shape of our science must be largely influenced by the Image of Man at its center. Say that man is good—and you have one kind of social theory; say that he is bad—and you have a philosophy that more or less determines how you will formulate your hypotheses about man and society.[5]

In *Beyond Alienation* Becker was even more blunt: "There is no theory about man without a belief in what is proper for man."[6]

Here Becker himself suggests an approach to his work consonant with a theology of culture. As noted in the introduction, a theology of culture is especially attentive to the master images and symbols at the centre of cultural activity. Science—including a "science of man"—is one such activity. Becker's "science of man" is a multidisciplinary quest for knowledge, guided by faith, with a normative image of human existence at its centre. This chapter is an exploration of that master image which Becker termed *homo poeta*.

This chapter begins with an examination of Becker's ontology, which sets the stage onto which humans will appear. It then commences a dialogue with what Becker sees as distinctive about humans among the other animals: that the human person is a meaning-creating animal. The place of such meaning-creating animals in a world striving after freedom and individuality shall be carefully noted. This sets up the central point discussed in the chapter: that Becker thus "names" the human person not *homo sapiens* but *homo poeta*. We shall see that *homo poeta* is an imagined, autonomous individual who is not reducible to any cultural role. Finally, questions about Becker's vision, especially concerning its depreciation of cultural life and its own reduction of the individual, will be raised.

An Ontology of Striving

Ontology is that branch of study which attempts to discern the basic structural features of existence. Laying bare the everyday world, it tries to discover and articulate how things "hang together." Ontology describes what may be called "the skin and bones of existence" which binds all creatures together. "In order to understand man, we must understand what he is striving for—not only as a member of society, not only as a unitary organism, but as a part of *nature*, as a dimension of life."[7] Becker saw that one could only ascertain what human beings were up to as "vehicles of the life force"[8] by taking note of the features of life—those fundamental motives of all creaturely life, and then by noting what made humans different.[9]

Life and the Life World

The Striving Character of "Life"

Becker contends that life is a unified, ongoing, forward-moving process of genesis and change. Organisms continue the life process by feeding themselves and perpetuating their species. Each obeys a simply formula: "See, place, move forward." As long as an organism is moving forward, we call it "alive." When it ceases to move forward, we usually call it "dead."[10] Viewed thus, every organism

> ... exists in a certain state of tension, a minus situation which it attempts constantly to overcome. No sooner is food ingested, waste excreted, satisfaction momentarily achieved, than the tension again begins to rise and equilibrium slips away.[11]

Even at a most basic level, organisms strive after satisfaction and control, " ... for a firmer grasp on the flux of experience."[12] A final grasp on experience is impossible, since without striving "there would be no organismic existence as we know it."[13] The unitary life process that all creatures participate in is *inherently* one of tension and striving. No sooner is satisfaction reached, food ingested or enemies destroyed than a new stimulus comes into the field of the organism, and upsets its momentary equilibrium.

But this dialectic of striving is not pointless or absurd. Becker wanted to avoid a paralyzing, fatalistic resignation. With each fleeting union with the world, newness and innovation are brought into being. "Momentary integrations," he writes, "are not ... a return to *former* equilibriums, but the creation of something new."[14] Hence the forward momentum of life is guaranteed by the very tensions threatening the security of every organism:

> In this kind of transaction, the organism and the world are in continued states of transformation. The organism comes into contact with the world, loses it, then comes into contact with it again in a different way.[15]

Hence life in process moves on and progresses in a rhythm of striving, unbalancing and integrating.[16]

The Life World

Every organism strives within a particular life world, or *umwelt*. This is a world of safe, dependable action in which each organismic species is uniquely equipped to act. On a pre-human level, *umwelten* are species-specific, differentiated in terms of the sensory array of each species.[17] The different sensory capabilities of a dog and a fly mean that each individual member of that species dwells in a "dog" world or a "fly" world.

Organisms are sensitive to objects, and to certain relations which obtain between objects and the organism itself. The differing sense apparatus of each species means that each life-world is populated by particular kinds of objects. These objects, in turn, call forth specific kinds of action from the organism. On a simple level—for example in that of an amoeba—a stimulus object enters the perceptual field of the creature, and the creature responds to this irritation by extending a pseudopod and ingesting it. This is integration on a basic level: organism and environment are integrated when the stimulus coming from that environment is incorporated into the experience of the organism.[18] Through responding to objects, the organism "behaves itself" into its world.

Action and Instinct

Progressive Freedom of Reactivity

Moving up the evolutionary scale, the sensory array of creatures becomes increasingly complex (such as the development of eyes, ears and nose) and thus the kinds of objects populating the various life-worlds change in character. Life-worlds increase in differentiation and richness with the development of ever more complex sensory arrays.

For Becker's amoeba, the choice is simple: either ingest the object, move away from it (if danger is sensed) or simply ignore it. But with increasing differentiation, there are a larger number of behavioural possibilities for a given stimulus. While this makes integration more complicated, it also means an enrichment in the object world of the organism.

Becker calls this differentiation "the progressive freedom of reactivity,"[19] and it provides the clue for evolutionary movement. Life is going somewhere; toward freedom. Freedom simply means having more options or projected actions to choose from.[20] And how does the animal "choose?" Becker claims that nature, in giving each organism a life-world to tame, provides preset patterns of behaviour, or "instincts." These instincts, as behavioural possibilities toward objects, together constitute "mind." When mind is brought to bear on the world, "meaning" is born.[21]

Organismic striving is motivated by a quest for safety and certainty. A threatening and chaotic world is converted into a safe and meaningful world as objects are apprehended. But since action is primary, apprehension is always active. In other words, "apprehending" an object refers to the way an organism "renders that object according to an intentional use." Becker calls this "abstraction.[22]

Abstraction

In converting the world into a meaningful environment through abstraction, the organism deals not with "whole objects" but with "part objects." The organism sees only the side of the object that it can act toward.[23] "Abstraction" refers to the way objects are characterized and classified according to usage.

An object in the field of the organism moves from subsistence to existence when it is constituted by a behavioural pattern.[24] Thus the only objects that exist for the organism are those it is able to react to. Hence the life worlds of "lower" animals are limited by their instinctual processes.

Summary: The Need for a New Stage in Evolution

Three features of Becker's ontology of striving come to the fore. First, if "all organisms are born to act,"[25] and if action is made possible by an object with certain qualities calling forth a response from the organism, and if objects are created and constituted in action—then it is evident that action and objects cohere in a self-reinforcing circle. If the essence of the life-force is one of striving motion, of challenge and mastery, then action integrates the organism with the rest of the world. This establishes for Becker the basic neutrality of organismic striving ... and the innocence of nature itself.

Second, on a pre-human level, meaning[26] and action, stimulus and response, potentiality and actuality, are inseparable. When action bogs down, it does so "into the surrender of death."

Third, also on a pre-human level, the organism is guided by intentionalities or instincts. The world is "inherently meaningful" and "eternally alive"[27] for such organisms. Yet this also means a closing down of innovation in life ... which for Becker is what gives life its "open" character of striving toward freedom. Even the most complex of pre-human animals is "enslaved to the properties" of the objects populating its life world.[28]

Becker's vision screens ingenuity out of the pre-human world. While he places more developed primates higher on the scale of "progressive freedom of reactivity,"[29] all animals on a pre-human level are restricted by instincts and hence operate with a finite (limited) number of possible actions. If the life process is striving for freedom, then a new emergent stage would have to come about. The pinnacle of evolution would have to be open and instinct free.

Firm Meaning: The Goal of Human Striving

It would not be an overstatement to say that the legacy of contemporary views of human existence owes more to the writings of Karl Marx and Sigmund Freud[30] than to any others. Much of Becker's writings are struggles with the legacy of these two figures for the human sciences. Characteristic of his critique of them was the way they failed to allow for human agency by making the person into an object—either of historical forces (Marx) or of biological drives (Freud). So despite Freud's insights into human developmental processes and the structure of morality, he

> ... was never more wrong than when he opined ... that "Dark, unfeeling and unloving powers determine human destiny...." Psychoanalytic theory pretended *to be* an integral science of man, but the epitaph for these imperialistic pretensions can be written in one brief sentence: Freud thought that man strives primarily for basic biological satisfaction, but *homo poeta* strives above all for firm meaning.[31]

This programmatic statement makes three points relevant here. First, human striving cannot be reduced to the outworking of forces of which the person is object. Second, human intentionality, what people strive after, is the proper focus of the "science of man." "Meaning" is the primary category of this science. Third, the "name" of humanity is *homo poeta*. This section begins by unpacking the phrase "firm meaning" which will open the way for an investigation of why Becker wishes to understand, or "name" humanity as *homo poeta*.

Meaning

Any biological account of human existence is bound to give only part of the human story. Human action differs from non-human action in that human actions have "meanings attached."[32] Using the term "attachment" qualifying "meanings" indicates that for Becker, on a human level, "meanings" are not inherent. Humanity has the task of "maximizing Being" and "Life" by maximizing its own being in the creation of "rich, deep and original human meanings."[33]

The Achievement of Meaning

Becker placed humanity at the pinnacle of emergent evolutionary development. "Life" seeks to actualize its being in and through humanity. The highest point of evolution is characterized by "openness," by freedom from instinctual patterns.[34] The corollary of this is that that which constricted organisms on the pre-human level had to be absent from humanity, namely, "natural drives" or instincts. It follows (given the previous discussion of the relationship between organism and environment) that the human person is born without a species-specific meaning world "given" by nature. Likewise it follows that the world is not "inherently meaningful" for this open creature. If we come into the world without our own space to occupy, then each person's task is to find a way into the world, to become part of it and to make a distinguishing mark upon it.

"Meaning" on a human level is something *achieved* rather than *given*, *created* rather than *discovered*. Unlike the lower animals, we have no preset place in the world, no space to call our own.[35] There is a fundamental absence at the core of the human creature, a space waiting to be filled. We are each born into a "minus situation" we must strive to overcome,[36] building ourselves into the world in weaving a tapestry of behavioural patterns through action.

Meaning and Self-Esteem

Human meanings are aimed toward "self-esteem" or "self-feeling."[37] That is, as each of us acts meaningfully upon the world, we come to *feel* part of a life world. But more than a part, we feel the world centred around us. We each discover ourselves as selves by experiencing the world responding to our actions.

Hence Becker's human may be described as self-conscious and self-reflexive. This idea of "self-esteem," to be discussed in more detail below, takes a crucial role in Becker's theory. Connecting it to organismic striving shows the essentially neutral nature of this striving after firm meaning. But while Becker understands striving "in itself" to be neither good nor evil, it is, however, never innocent. It is always *directed*. Thus our ways of gaining a sagacious sense of self can be good or bad. This point will be elaborated on below.

Meaning and Mastery

For Becker, "firm" meaning is tied in with "mastery" words and phrases, such as "rendering predictable," "manipulation" and "control." And yet all of these have qualifications placed on them. Control is carefully distinguished from "coercion" and predictability from "rigidification." Why? Because for Becker, all human action must carry life further. Coercion strips the thing or person acted upon of its own individuality, its own subjectivity. And a rigidified human world closes off possibility and hence the movement of life toward the new.

Thus far Becker's claim that the creature *qua* creature strives for a firm grasp on its world has been noted. Objects are rendered predictable for organisms on a pre-human level through instincts. On the human level this predictability must be sought in a socially created meaning scheme. Predictability involves both objects and action. The objects around each person must be rendered in such a way as to grant the possibility of safe action. Only in this way can persons sense whether an object in their field is dangerous or friendly. It must be fitted into a meaning scheme.

Predictability also concerns the calling forth of action. Each person needs to know what an acceptable response is within a given situation. *Conventions* guide behaviour in such a way as it will not be viewed as threatening by others. They provide a clear path of action in the world. The socially staged drama grants each individual a role, a part to play. There is a range of actions appropriate, for example, to a doctor that would not be appropriate to a scholar or a bus driver. This is both good and bad for Becker. It is *good* in that we do indeed need to know what our role is in the world. It is *bad* in that the temptation to rigidify the world and to reduce the individual to a static role is always present.

Put another way, "predictability"—knowing what role others play and what role the self is to play—describes the world of "safety and security." This all functions to grant each of us a sense that *within* a safe and secure house, we are master. To lose control is to lose the ability to act meaningfully. As in the pre-human world, to stop acting is to bog down in the surrender of death. Becker's self is a self "in control."[38]

If "firm meaning" is what we are really striving for, then firmness is also something contrived, created as a function of control. The world, Becker says, is a chaotic mass of sensation before it is ordered by the self. Firm meaning then is a behavioural "ordering" of sensation.[39]

Meaning and Contingency

Although no particular meaning is "necessary," it is nonetheless necessary, as Becker sees it, that we create meaning. Meaning is as requisite for human function-ing as food and shelter. In fact, as Becker says, it is more so. Without meaning, we cannot act. Without action, we cease to exist. As noted above, each person must get his or her patterns of action, their "cues," as it were, from society.

But humanly created meaning is inherently precarious. This is so, not only because it is always open to being undermined by further experience,[40] but precisely because it is *constructed*. The precariousness of human meaning is founded, for Becker, on the very openness allowing us to go beyond the constrictions of instinct driven animals. Meaning is constructed out of "symbolic stuff," out of words. Since words bear no necessary relation to "reality," human meanings[41] are radically *contingent*. This is why Becker calls them "fictions" and "games." Becker saw this as the great discovery of the Enlightenment. Criticism of social organizations and structures presupposes such contingency.

So precarious are our meaning schemes,[42] and yet so necessary, that we defend them at all costs. To allow them to be criticized is to subject them to undermining. To relativize them by placing them alongside other meaning schemes is to question their finality. Without firm meaning we stand naked before threaten-ing and chaotic nature. Each meaning scheme has to carry enough conviction that its subjects see it as real, as simply "the way things are."[43]

The Alienated Modern Consciousness

To this point, what Becker sees humans as striving after ("firm meaning"), and what he means by it have been elucidated. Human presence in the world is based on a fundamental absence, a basic sense of homelessness. We are perpetual "home makers," fashioning our dwellings by creating meaning worlds to inhabit. We do this as creatures, however. In other words, humans fashion their world, and themselves, in relation to and interaction with "nature." At all times the dialectical, moving, striving character of life must be maintained.

This world has to provide security through predictability, it must merge convincingly with the natural, and it must allow for human control. Each of these is precarious. Predictability can degenerate into life as "one damn thing after another." Conviction can overlook the hard world of things in favour of the ethereal symbol. Control can coerce.

The creation of meaning is a precarious task. This is true not just for humans in general, but for modern humans in particular. But is Becker's insight not more applicable to the latter than the former? Does Becker simply universalize the experience of modern humanity, expanding it into a broad anthropology embracing all humans? Indeed his accounting of humans as open creatures, natively "empty" but striving for fulfilment, parallels the situation of moderns depicted as striving for an integral world picture in which to act. The decline of the medieval world picture (where everyone was born into a social situation where role and place were already dictated for them) has not brought about a coherent successor picture. Since moderns experience themselves as alienated, it is not surprising that a modern person defines the human condition as alienated.

Becker also merges the human and the animal by saying that we are open *creatures*. While not having a native world to act in, we nevertheless belong to the earth, to nature, to life. Human striving after meaning must be done as a part of the *life process*. The world that we are called to act upon is the world of nature. Once again the alienated modern consciousness makes an appearance in Becker. If we have to act on nature in order to feel ourselves a part of nature, then it is strongly implied that we are not natively a part of nature, that we are strangers in a strange land, foreigners.

Self-esteem

If firm meaning indicates what Becker means by human, underneath all externalities of culture and convention, the question remains: what lies beneath this striving? What is it that drives the striving after firm meaning?

All life seeks to maintain something Becker calls "self-feeling." Becker calls this "self-esteem" when he speaks of it in reference to humans. The crucial difference is that pre-human organisms are already built into their world. Self-feeling is earned by realizing something already given, in action. For humanity there is no such "given" world. Self-esteem then is constructed symbolically in a social meaning scheme.

Anxiety

It would be short-circuiting Becker's theory simply to say that self-esteem is the primary human motivator. Self-esteem is precipitated by something else: organismic anxiety. For animals anxiety is simply a tension between contact surface and inner intentions which is resolved in action. The threat to mastery is overcome in satisfying action.

For humans, says Becker, mastery is not an original problem. For the infant, the world is the mother. And that world is organismic, physical, warm and nurturing. Mother devotes all her attention to the infant. When the growing child realizes that mother has a separate existence, and that it has a physical body (the functions of which can either attract or repulse the mother), it becomes faced with the problem of how to maintain that early feeling. The child has to learn to *please* mother through controlling or mastering the body and its functions. And yet this mastery must be done on mother's terms: she makes the rules for the disposal of bodily functions, she directs the child to the "potty." Meaningfully acting on the stirring in its bowels involves "sitting on the cold porcelain thing." This pleases mother and carries forth the child's self-esteem.

As mother tends to other things the child has to face "going it alone." This is good, in that the child must individuate if it is to be human. Part of being human is the detachment from the "determined" world of bodies to allow remerging with it in new ways. But detachment is bad because the child learns it can no longer carry forth self-esteem in bodily connection with mother. New ways to carry forth self-esteem must be found.

Becker is saying that the developing person emerges as an individual by finding their own style of merging with the world. This is what Alfred Adler called "life style."[44] Becker adds the point that this life style must always answer to the social setting that emerging individuals find themselves in. Perhaps this point could be put metaphorically by saying that all persons write their own variation on the cultural theme learned in development. This variation is however an unauthentic one since it deals with problems set up in a "given" situation. It is a function of disempowerment.

The Oedipal Transition

The myth of *Oedipus Rex* has fascinated Enlightenment thinkers from Hegel to Freud. Claiming that basic human motives were sexual in nature, and that the infant sustained an "erotic" relation with mother, Freud saw the stages in the relation exhibited in various zones which became "charged" with sexual energy. Individuation was founded on a growing frustration which eventually turned the infant away from mother.

Becker thought that Freud saw human emergence as determined, since he saw the forces impelling development as "biological" or "instinctual." We are "subject to" these forces. For Becker, the human was tasked by the life force toward individuation. But this individuation is always qualified by the need to deal with anxiety by maintaining self-esteem.

Becker reinterprets Freud's categories "anal," "oral" and "phallic" as sites where the drive to individuation bogs down. They describe the tension of the developing child caught between moving beyond mother and learning new ways of maintaining self-esteem, and staying back and continuing to earn the warm feeling of nurture from mother. The Oedipal transition describes the time at which the child learns to relate to mother (and hence to the physical world), as father relates.[45] Rather than dealing with bodily orifices, it learns to deal with symbols.

Having passed through the Oedipal phase, the child is trained to act in the cultural world it has seen father acting in. This world is one of detachment and individuality ("freedom") rather than warm bodily nurture ("determinism"). Living in this world involves internalizing the rules and obligations that heretofore have been "imposed" by father's belt and slippers. The child learns to say, "There is no longer any need to punish me, father; I will punish myself now." The child *becomes* father by internalizing father's role.

The Gendered Dimensions of the Oedipal Transition

Becker thought that he was speaking in universal terms when he gave his interpretation of individuation. Certainly if the tenets of his theory are accepted—and bearing in mind that theory as an accounting of certain aspects of the structure of existence tends to have a universal thrust—his interpretation makes sense. For if what makes humans different from animals is that they are born open rather than into a species-specific meaning world, then reference to the human person must be in terms of "the individual," rather than "the species." While there is a "dog" world and a "fly" world, for Becker there is no such thing as a "human" world. There are only human "worlds." Nevertheless all human worlds have common features. One of those is that they all have some version of the Oedipal transition.

But Becker also speaks out of a particular situation. He does his interpretation from a standpoint. This is exhibited in a very important assumption that his view of individuation makes. It may be stated propositionally thus: as male is to female, so culture is to nature. As Jessica Benjamin has pointed out, the Oedipal myth itself has been interpreted in such a way as to legitimize the socially constructed roles of male and female in the modern world.[46]

While it may be less true now than it was in Becker's time, men remain the progenitors of culture. Women are (still largely) trained as tending the home and providing a warm and nurturing environment for men. This is a critical point to make, since it underscores a conservative, socially legitimizing strand in Becker's supposedly "radical" theory.

Staging the Self

Becker's view of the urge to self-esteem as the primary human motive explained for him the mystery of early human development. It also accounted for the nature of human sociality.

Sociality as Problem

The key assumption that Becker makes in all his discussions of sociality is this: individuality defines the self over against others. Put linguistically, the word "I" takes shape over against all others named "not I." Individuality is grounded in separation from others. Paradoxically, individuals are fated to derive self-esteem from those same others.

Yet self-esteem is, like "meaning," inherently precarious because it is contrived. Every encounter with an other is a possible undermining of self-esteem, as well as a possible enhancement of it. How can individuals be brought together without destroying self-esteem? How can an individual function alongside other individuals, without losing the primary sense of value in the world?[47] Becker thought that providing an answer to these questions was the task of *culture*.[48]

Learning the Lines: Deference and Demeanour

A culture must keep two things in tension if it is to function as preserver of self-esteem. First: it must protect the privacy of the individual self, to keep it from being invaded by others. Second, culture must allow for social interaction within which the individual may not only be included, but experience mastery.

Cultures fulfil these tasks by means of a heavily ritualized, intricate web of rules and conventions. This web gives space, establishes boundaries and yet also allows for interaction. Following Erving Goffman's influential *The Presentation of the Self in Everyday Life*,[49] Becker uses two key terms in describing this framework. The first term is "deference." Deferential rules take two forms. In the first, termed "rituals of avoidance," the self is protected from the invasion of others by conventions that keep them at a distance. For example, on a bus an unspoken rule prevents a man from violating the space of the woman sitting next to him by pouring out his life story. In the second, termed "rituals of presentation," my right to engage the other is established. "Rituals of avoidance" recognize the self as personal. "Rituals of presentation" recognize the self as social.[50]

The second key term Becker uses is "demeanour," and this is where the whole interactive social framework can be compromised. For demeanour refers to the task of every person to present to the other what Becker calls "a transactable self." Each person must bring a self to the encounter, a self capable of calling forth response from the other. Becker also calls this the task of "presenting a credible stage personality."[51] If someone's "stage personality" is not credible, then the other either will not recognize them, or will be made uncomfortable enough to stall the interaction. In sum, social rules make it possible for a person to risk his or her self-esteem in the encounter with an other. They also call upon the person, reciprocally, to protect the self-esteem of the other. The presentation of the self is done in terms of mediating formulas (such as "How are you?" "Good to see you!" and "See you later") which permit interaction between individuals.

Power, Language and Identity
The meaning context for social interaction is therefore a linguistic one. But it must also facilitate the experience of control over the other for the sake of enhancing the self. And so saying "hello" or "thank you" to the other asserts the self and requires the other to respond appropriately. In creating such a meaning context, we create and renew ourselves, our identities. An identity, that is, is validated by the fact that one person has "caused" another to respond "meaningfully."

For Becker, identity is nothing more than "the measure of power and participation of the individual in the joint cultural staging of self-enhancing ceremony."[52] Power, language and identity are part of a self-reinforcing circle that, for Becker, social interaction sets in motion. Someone lacking an identity will not bring anything to the interaction, and it will stall. An experience of power (which again, for Becker, is always "power over") is the ability to manipulate the linguistic context, knowing the "rules," expressing proper deference and demeanour. Power over others consists in presenting, as Becker puts it, "an infallible self," and in commanding dexterous performance of deference.

The Economics of Self-Esteem
While Becker's economic metaphors serve to illuminate somewhat the experience of the self in society, they are also problematic. They tend to present social interaction in terms of a "steady state" economy in which the machinery is kept in balance by adjustments of distributional resources. Self-esteem is a scarce resource which must be purchased and used in such a way as to keep everything in motion and in proper balance. This accounts for Becker's view of culture as essentially conservative, and why he sees it as closing down human spontaneity and possibility. Culture represses individuality, and therefore freedom. Given this logic, Becker's conclusion is inescapable: culture reinstinctivizes human individuals by enslaving them to a given world.[53]

Why culture, then? According to Becker, culture is a mechanism of compensation whereby the human animal compensates for its inherent deficiency of instincts and its natural inferiority to other animals. Becker derived this view not from empirical investigation but from post-Freudian psychology and anthropology.[54] Culture is a covering, a defense mechanism where individuals band together to

assert collectively what they cannot assert individually: control over the environment. Individuals give away their control to the "herd" in order to get back security
and self-esteem. This assumes that culture is not native to human existence, that it
is a mere covering that can be shed once the individual is strong enough to face the
cold, naked. It shall become evident below that this view got Becker into much
difficulty.

Summary and Transition to Homo Poeta

The previous section discussed Becker's reinterpretation of Freud's view of
the Oedipus complex in terming it "the Oedipal transition" and by claiming that it
refers to learning to master anxiety, within the family context, as a response to the
need to differentiate and individuate, while carrying forth self-esteem. This involves
a shift from the warm, nurturing affirmation of value by mother to the cold, symbolic
affirmation of father. On the other side of the Oedipal transition, culture provides
a symbolic context for action, a way of getting the self into the world, of allowing the
self to feel its manipulatory power over others. Self-esteem is carried forth and
individuality is strengthened, even as it is protected.

But there is a negative side to this as well. In order to receive support
(self-esteem), each individual needs to legitimize a particular, cultural, linguistic
"web" which enables connection with others. Difficulties with this view have already
become apparent, specifically the way Becker's metaphor is slanted toward a view
of culture as closing down and restricted. How does all this relate to this work?

As an Enlightenment man, Becker is profoundly uncomfortable with "the
given." Whether a social system, a family situation or a life style, the given is precisely
what is criticizable. If all cultural worlds are "given" worlds in the static way that
Becker understands them, then as long as we find our agency, our identity, in a
particular narrow cultural world, we are enslaved. Put another way, the well-encul-
turated actor is no closer to freedom as Becker defines it than the instinct-driven
automatons in nature. The actor takes cues from a limited repertoire of acceptable
behaviours.

At bottom, when the veneer of cultural "appearances" is stripped away, this
is all we are left with. Culture renders objects in such a way as to make them safe
to act on. Normative language, or talk of "right" and "wrong," is simply an alternative way of saying "this" object or "that" action are not recognized and hence will
not enhance self-esteem. This object or that action is deemed taboo if it does not
contribute to the joint staging of meaning, if it does not carry the meaning plot
forward.[55]

The recovery of individuality then must consist in the reassertion of the
individual over against the culture. We each must come to redefine ourselves,
becoming our own creator, spinning out our own life as a very particular poetry.
Becker calls this envisioned human person *homo poeta*.

Homo Poeta as Normative Model of Human Becoming

A vision, says James Olthuis, has a dual focus. It functions both *descriptively* and *normatively*.[56] Ernest Becker held a similar view, saying that the vision of humanity that his science centred around not only sought to describe human intentionality, but to prescribe an "ideal type" or model for humanity. Such a model became even more essential for Becker since he claimed that humanity had not yet fully "arrived," that humanity was in a continual state of becoming.[57] An ideal type, then, is a concrete model of *what* humanity is (or "ought" to be) becoming.

Good Art and Bad Art

Becker used the metaphor of the "artist" to prescribe what humanity was becoming. While a category like "aesthetics" in the work of a social scientist might seem curious, it enabled him to account for why so many were unfulfilled: their art was "twisted." It also enabled him to pronounce judgment on "cultural humans": they stamped the world with sameness.

The Category of the Aesthetic[58]

The weaving of fictions into the world in which the symbol becomes experienced as the real is termed by Becker "aesthetics."[59] *Homo poeta* is an artist called continually to reshape the world into newer patterns, an activity which creates "values" reflecting "man's possession of the world."[60] In the active fusion of symbolic meaning and organismic world the person attains conviction and the world comes alive. Becker describes this dynamic in different ways:

> ... the human condition (is) the *esthetic transcendence* of natural accident, of *indifferent* fate.[61]

> When man creates his own meaning he takes possession of the world, ... he makes an esthetically significant panorama out of a gray, neutral world.[62]

> ... man becomes truly man by the esthetic transformation of the world with his free, directive energies.[63]

"Nature" is depicted by Becker as "fate," as "gray" and as "indifferent." Neither values nor meaning can be read out of nature.[64] "Brute nature" is a backdrop against which *homo poeta* spins out meaning. This echoes Becker's conviction that humans are not born into a world, but a backdrop. The depreciation of "the natural" in Becker is stark. It is also very modern.[65]

Becker's metaphor tells us that humanity relates to nature the way an artist relates to his or her material. The artist takes material and chisels, shapes and defines it. The artist gives it his or her own unique "twisting." As an artist, *homo poeta* brings newness into the world by "adding to nature what she only sparingly gives: symbolic significance."[66]

It is this impulsion to create the new that carries human life forward. We can only experience "[our] own being in a dialogue with nature."[67] In doing so we place ourselves on the "cutting edge" of the evolutionary process. It is this process, Becker urges, that calls us continually to remake the world, to break old forms and to carry the process onward.

Twisted Persons

But it is not only the world of nature that is given a "twist" by human artistic activity. This also applies to *homo poeta*. As we saw in our examination of Becker's view of the Oedipal transition, his view of the human person is that everyone is created by a process of socialization which begins in the family and is cumulated in culture. Culture encloses the world and the self. Culture enslaves the individual.

Becker's vision of *homo poeta* is set over against "cultural humans." *Homo poeta* is an individual corresponding to no species, no set narrowing of the world. Becker's point could be stated this way: the individual understood as *homo poeta* is a species unto itself, indwelling an *umwelt* of its own creation. "Cultural people" on the other hand are mere variations on a cultural theme, enslaved to the herd, receiving cues from others.

Homo poeta functioned for Becker as a normative type in his earlier writings. It is important to realize that Becker's "social phenomenology"[68] sought to understand what all people everywhere were doing when they acted. In Becker's view, everyone was fashioning their life as a work of art. Unfortunately, not everybody is a good artist.

Fetishism

The fetishist typifies "bad aesthetics" for Becker. Whether the individual can attain aesthetic fusion with the world depends on whether the person has strength to act on whole objects, with their own mystery. To do this means loosening up the accepted form of the objects, that is, the particular way culture has "rendered" them. Strength is necessary to act on whole objects. Lacking such strength, acting in accepted safety, necessitates fetishism.[69]

Fetishism is usually associated with sexual practices, as when a person uses boots or corsets as aids to masturbation. Becker uses the term "fetishism" in related but different ways. First, he sees it as a manifestation of the basic problem of organismic action. All humans fetishize "by nature." We must act on objects, and those objects must be rendered in such a way as to allow action as part of an integral scheme of meaning. Abstraction, as demonstrated above, is done by all animals, and all humans, in action.[70]

Becker also uses fetishism as a critical concept. Low self-esteem condemns the weak person to fear acting on whole objects. Such a person is forced to reduce further the object to something else, something from which a response can be coerced. There is nothing *inherently* sexual about a boot. However when the fetishist conceives a magical connection between it and sexual organs, it becomes a substitute for actual sexual interaction with another person. The fetishist must "rob" the object, rather than "transact" with it. Put more bluntly, the fetishist is a rapist rather than a lover in relation to the object.

In the absence of a unified meaning scheme, the person may see the world through fetish objects: a woman, a bank balance, academic grades. The world of significance becomes reduced to such objects, and life is consumed by their daily pursuit. When fetishism reaches this level, Becker calls it "fetishizing the life force."[71] This represents the lowest point that humans (given their place in the evolutionary process) can reach.

One of the difficulties in reading Becker on fetishism is that he uses the term in all three ways, without making explicit distinctions. Thus he condemns modern consumer society as fetishistic because of the shallowness of its meaning games, while in the same writing saying that fetishism is a feature of human existence as such. And yet he praises so-called "primitive" societies precisely because, unlike industrial ones, they *don't* fetishize. Fetishism is at the same time a developmental problem caused by particular socialization practices, and an structural problem integrally related to *any* socialization practice. I will return to this critical point below.

The Conversion to Authenticity

Just as there is good and bad art, and the development of such art depends on the quality of the training of the artist, as well as the materials available, so there are authentic and inauthentic humans. But just as artists are "made" and not born, so "authentic humanity" arises out of the dust of inauthentic humanity. How does this happen?

The Problem of Strength

Whether fetishists by nature or by nurture, we are all "by nature" left with the problem of how to attain authenticity. The problem of strength is a problem of conversion. The question is how the well enculturated actor (which by definition we all are until we reach "authenticity") is to move toward individuality and authenticity. While "to offer up new meanings is to give birth, to bring the unknown into the world,"[72] "this process of birth, ... cutting oneself off from society is a choice for potential self-annihilation or non being."[73]

"Courage" is prerequisite to such a conversion. Courage is needed to face the void that envelopes the person who dares create the new. But if everyone is dependent on others for a feeling of self-value, where will such courage come from? Moreover, if creating new meanings reawakens the anxiety which the early socialization process "tamed" (such that the individual has already been "deprived of a belief in his or her own powers"),[74] where will the strength come from to deal with this anxiety? This problem would plague Becker for the rest of his writing career, for it concerned the very possibilities for realizing his vision of *homo poeta*.

Critical Reason

Salvation for the modern person comes in understanding the particular socialization process to which they have been subjected. This in-sight comes through what Becker termed "critical reason." It involves seeing-through how the self has been reduced to a role in a culturally contingent drama.

Critical reason addresses the problem of anxiety in this way: "We cannot be anxious about that which we truly understand." And so the strength to be freed up for creation of new meanings "requires a cognitive grasp of one's situation."[75] Becker was convinced that this was a matter of education.

It is therefore not surprising that for Becker the key area of social change was the university, which was potentially "the handmaiden of life itself."[76] And yet contemporary university education had lost its nerve, more concerned with preparing people to be uncritical cogs in a military-industrial machine. In the critical awareness of the sixties, Becker saw possible a generation of students raised to be critics of the ways things were in their day, with the university seeking "to unfold the universal man, the man free from the automatic constraints of his own culture and times."[77] All that had to be done was to make knowledge self-critical:

> "Know thyself," know what prevents you from being "self-reliant." Know how you were deprived of the ability to make your own judgments; know how the worldview of your society was built into your perceptions; know how those who trained you to see and think, literally placed themselves into your mind; know how they became the self upon your self, the "superego" upon your "ego," the voice of conscience whispering behind your voice.[78]

Social Self and Whole Objects

Self-awareness only gives a part of the human salvation story. There is still the matter of human sociality. Becker saw that individuals would always require some validation for their meanings, an awareness that those meanings were part of some larger scheme or purpose. And yet it was this very tendency to seek validation that led to symbolic reinstinctivization in society. Any scheme or purpose therefore would have to be one that allowed individuality and spontaneity.

Becker thought that it was in the validating power of the intersubjective encounter, where each one "allows" the other the right to their own meanings, that the foundation for an ideal society could be found. Such a society would be the antithesis of the present narrowing one where individuals are reduced to roles, as players in an arbitrarily conceived drama. In Becker's ideal society, individuals have been freed to relate to others as whole objects,[79] rather than part objects. This key distinction between "part" and "whole" objects needs clarification.

As already noted, Becker thought our uncritical allegiance to the system of meaning we are born into provides safety and security. Unpredictable and spontaneous person-objects around the individual become predictable as they are related to in terms of role and status. The individual knows what is expected by others, and *vice versa*, based on the part each plays in the cultural fiction. Unthinkingly, we relate to others only in terms of the role they play. They are part and not whole objects.

By a "whole" object, Becker means the irreducible aspect of the individual. While the individual is formed in the matrix of society, the individual is not reducible to social constructs. Becker asserted that the individual is always greater than his or her social self. He says this because to deny it (as he had hinted in 1962)[80] would be to deny the possibility of change and legitimize, even normalize, enslavement of the individual by society. It is precisely this "greater than" that social fictions strive to keep in check. At the same time this "greater than" is the individuality that one brings to the world, his or her distinctive gift.[81]

By "part object" Becker refers to the social self, which is a reduction of the individual to a role. While we need social conventions, which provide a safe and predictable world, they also hinder the social encounter which, says Becker, is the locus for the greatest liberation of the life force. Why is this? Because the encounter with another human person is an encounter with mystery, with the unknowable and the irreducible.

The Reassertion of Autonomy

Curiously, however, Becker never goes on to develop this intersubjective vision as the basis for society.[82] Relationality is *not* the basis for society. It is the need for individuals to maintain self-esteem that is. Society is an aggregate of individuals, and *die soziale frage*,[83] the bond between individuals, consists in an economy of self-esteem. Society exists, normatively, for the sake of the individual. The *telos* of culture is to "cultivate" individuals. In fact, Becker reasserts the theme of individual autonomy when he claims that "the forces of nature are embodied in the individual spirit."[84] Society functions to provide the space for individual autonomy.[85]

Criticisms of Homo Poeta

Metaphors (or images) open up new aspects of life. They also close down other aspects of life. This is why they are continually in need of reform(ul)ation. The image of humanity as *poet* or *artist* is like this. Becker's imagining humanity as *homo poeta* is open to critique in that it suppresses other aspects of human life, reducing them to it. For instance, does it really honour ethical activity by reducing it to an "expression" of human artistic sensibility?

Criticism could also be levelled at the image of humanity as *homo poeta* on the basis of whether it doesn't "slight the darker side" of human activity. Indeed in his later work Becker himself voices this critique. Does saying that Hitler was a bad artist and the Nazi social creation of meaning was "shallow" (as if Becker were reviewing a play) honour the memory of suffering of those who were "rendered" by it? Is such a cool assessment appropriate to a philosophy professing to be humanistic?

But the criticisms in the present work are more interested in examining Becker's way of seeing. To change the metaphor slightly, it is in the way that the tradition within which Becker stands governs his sightline that is of significance. Sighting humanity as *homo poeta* is an function of Becker's Enlightenment vision: a vision which focuses upon autonomy as *the* normative human trait. This last section shall therefore begin with a criticism of the autonomous self posted by Becker, before briefly mentioning two other problems.

The Ambiguities of Autonomy

In pre-modern times, the idea of an autonomous self would have been impossible to grasp. As Bob Goudzwaard notes, the structure of medieval society was like the cathedral that stood in the middle of each city: rising from the lowly serf to the landlord and up to the church government, the cathedral enshrined the social structure as pointing up to heaven.[86] Everyone knew their place in this social order. As long as everyone kept their place, they were saved. Roles were static, hardened. One was "born into" one's place in the world.

Becker's critique of the reduction of the self to role (and his affirmation of the goal of autonomous self-creation)—founded as it is on the Enlightenment overthrow of the previous social order—is good in that it honours the self as dynamic and becoming, whereas roles tend to see the self as a static and fixed essence. Becker's observation that to see the self as a mere aggregate of roles closes the self down and confines agency within a structure of stimulus-response—that observation is an important critique of hierarchical institutions and societies.

Becker, however, goes too far in disconnecting the role self (that is, the particular part one plays in a particular society) from the actual self. Roles are, in his view, to be negated and thrown off for the sake of liberation. They are *de facto* unauthentic precisely because they are culturally "given." Since the self, in order to be authentic, must continually divest itself from its roles, Becker's theory is left with an impoverished individual, stripped of concrete identity with which to relate to the other.

Perhaps Becker's theory could be corrected by asserting that the role self can be a disclosure of the self in a particular situation, rather than a suppression of the self. This would be difficult for Becker to accept, however, since it would require him to take a very unmodern view of the self. He would have to find a way of seeing the self as always situated and bounded within a "given" world. Becker has already voiced the opinion of modernity in claiming that there is no given, except that which enslaves the individual. On Becker's view this enslavement is "necessary" because the individual is forced to uphold a cultural fiction or else face the void. To talk of "role" then is inevitably to disclose the self as enslaved.

This is not to say that Becker's self is not in fact situated. The autonomous self is situated dialectically—as Becker in his later theory would be forced to realize. Becker's self is caught within at least two impossible either/ors: the master-slave dialectic and something which may be referred to as the gift-call dialectic.[87] Each dialectic posits one pole as founded on the repression of the other pole.

As Jessica Benjamin has noted, the master-slave dialectic forms the context for modern views of the self.[88] We are either social victims ("cultural") or masters of our destiny ("authentic"). In asserting one side of this, the other side is lost.[89] And yet, because the suppression of the other pole leaves our humanity impoverished, we struggle against its complete suppression. Hence we can understand why an individualist like Becker tries valiantly to recover the social creation of meaning. However, since the only authentic "meaning" that he can affirm is "autonomy," Becker can only see society as a breeding and strengthening ground for individuals.

The gift-call dialectic is similar. Living according to "gift," in which we experience meaning in a given world, involves trading off our "authenticity" as Becker defines it. But Becker's alternative, which is living according to "call" (in which we continually and restlessly fashion and re-fashion ourselves), is oriented toward an undefinable and vacuous freedom.[90]

Both sets of opposites—master-slave and gift-call—are connected in that they suppress any deep human connectivity with other humans, or with creation. Yes, there are the webs of significance we spin, but at the end of the day *we* have to have spun them if we are to avoid being their victims.

And so it is questionable whether at the other end of self-criticism Becker's individual is any better off. Any identity ascribed to an individual, before critical self-consciousness is attained, is negated. People are forced by critical reason to regard themselves as victims of society. The achievement of autonomy means that each person stands over and against their own past, their own history. This is a form of alienation that denies the continuity of a person's life—and a supreme irony for someone who wrote a book claiming that a truly autonomous self would move "beyond alienation!"[91]

This ought not to be surprising, given the religious roots of Becker's tradition. After all, as Stanley Hauerwas has (with characteristic irony) pointed out, alienation is the chief moral virtue within Enlightenment liberalism.[92] The Enlightenment sought to empty the self of all particularity, to strip away our masks, in order to arrive at the bare truth. It is this "naked" self that is called "free": this nondescript (for descriptions also limit) evacuated and alienated self.

Perhaps there is irony here too, for the Enlightenment discovered (or constructed) "the individual," and in seeking to oppose alienation for the sake of the individual, actually deepened it. And so the modern self is bankrupt. It is, in the terms of Robert Lifton, a *protean self*.[93] It is a self that, sliding in and out of its roles without any one role to define it, truly is homeless. Becker began his description of humanity as homemaker. The present exposition draws to a close with modern humanity as homeless.

The Normalization of Brokenness

Above it was demonstrated that Becker's use of the term "fetish" is confusing. Beneath this confusion, however, lies a deeper problem. Becker confuses structural issues with developmental issues. Talking about fetishism as the way that humans "by nature" act on the world is a case of the former use. Talking about fetishism as "learned behaviour," as a *result* of low self esteem or as a consequence of modern society's lack of an integral centre and shared purpose is a case of the latter use.[94]

The consequences of this confusion are crucial, for it forces Becker to conclude that all human development is already broken *by definition*. All human formation is malformation. All direction is misdirection. Until, that is, the individual learns of this and adopts "autonomy" as norm.

This works against Becker's attempt to present the structural conditions of life as essentially neutral and humanity as malleable and open. It has the function of making brokenness a necessary precondition of authenticity. And so Becker, who was passionately committed to the causes that led students at his university into the streets in protest, can never radically condemn brokenness with any consistency. It is part of the process. Brokenness is normalized.[95]

If this is the accounting for evil that Becker thought we needed in order to bring about humanity's apotheosis, it is a great disappointment. For if authenticity is predicated on fallenness, if "good" is predicated on "evil" and (to return to the discussion above) freedom is predicated on slavery, there is no reason to condemn the Hitlers of this world. Nor is there a reason to hope for a world in which people don't have to go through hell in order to arrive at heaven.[96]

The Dialectics of Freedom

Becker saw that while history was "the record of the flowering of the human personality,"[97] and that "what urges man on is the unity of meaning and the need to maximize that meaning,"[98] history is a dialectic of constriction and autonomy, of opening up and closing down.

The truly free man is something we will always have to work toward; choices can never be as broad as we would like, nor fear and constriction ever banished.[99]

While "the innovator is the instrument of evolution itself"[100] which carries the life process onward, the innovator is set over and against culture which narrows life down:

> This is the dialectic of human freedom, the tension between an animal who needs a symbolically constituted sense of self-value and a society which, in granting it, reduces the individual to the slavery of habit and a narrow world view.[101]

This chapter began by noting Becker's ontology of striving, in which life is seen as a grand process carried forward by striving, unbalancing and integrating. The creative individual, located within this ontology and characterized as innovator for the life process, will therefore *always* have to have a something to lever his or her striving. The creative individual necessarily exists in tension with society. Likewise societies, if they are to survive, will always have to have dissident voices to prevent them from hardening.

Need and the Other

But what of the innovator, the creative genius? Where is such a "one" to find support for his ongoing creation of meaning? If the innovator is moving away from society in his or her acts of creation, and indeed negating his or her own "shaping" history, from whence comes support? This is another question with which Becker was occupied throughout his career. In *The Revolution in Psychiatry* (1964) he thought that the "other" that was addressed was the love object.[102] In *The Structure of Evil*, Becker comes to see that no "other" could bear the brunt of being placed in a position of validating meanings. He said that "man has to trust some divine purpose working itself out in history."[103] In other words, God is posited to fill the need of the person struggling for autonomy. The next chapter explores the transformations in Becker's work that this reassertion of God brought forth.

Notes

1. James H. Olthuis, "On Worldviews," in *Stained Glass: Worldviews and Social Science* (Lanham: University Press of America, 1989), 26.
2. The term "science of man" is frequently used by Becker. It is used both in a general (encompassing the disciplinary area of the so-called "human sciences" such as anthropology, psychology and sociology) and in a special sense (of a single discipline

embodying the Enlightenment vision). Because Becker uses the term here in the latter sense I place it in quotes.

3. For an illuminating analysis of modern science and its place in western society see Lesslie Newbigin, *Foolishness to the Greeks: The Gospel and Western Culture* (Grand Rapids: Eerdmans, 1986), ch. 2. Mary Midgley's *Science as Salvation: A Modern Myth and its Meaning* (London: Routledge, 1992) is also important in this regard.

4. *Beyond Alienation* (New York: George Braziller, 1967), 254.

5. *Angel in Armor* (New York: George Braziller, 1969), 159. It is important to note however that Becker was inconsistent in upholding this thesis. Just a few pages later (on 161) he claims that science *is* after all neutral. Even more curious, on 171 he claims that human "innocence" can be empirically demonstrated by looking at children "without preconceptions."

6. *Beyond Alienation*, 127.

7. *Beyond Alienation*, 169.

8. *Beyond Alienation*, 170.

9. See *Beyond Alienation*, 168-78 and *The Structure of Evil* (New York: George Braziller, 1968), 167-210.

10. *The Birth and Death of Meaning* (New York: Free Press of Glencoe, 1962), 33; *The Revolution in Psychiatry* (New York: Free Press of Glencoe, 1964), 11; *Angel in Armor*, 8.

11. *Revolution*, 34.

12. *Revolution*, 230.

13. *Revolution*, 231.

14. *Revolution*, 231.

15. *Revolution*, 231.

16. *Revolution*, 16. Integration, as will be shown, becomes an increasingly complex matter further up the evolutionary scale. A simple organism is satisfied more easily than one with "more complex receptors." Ibid, 34.

17. *Birth and Death*, 15.

18. *Revolution*, 34.

19. *Birth and Death*, 20. "Freedom of reactivity," is a curious expression. It seems to combine opposites: reactivity (determinism) and agency (freedom).

20. For Becker's view of freedom, see *Beyond Alienation*, 170-74.

21. *Revolution*, 12-13.

22. *Revolution*, 24-27.

23. Becker seems to envision organisms relating to objects in a way similar to a technician relating to a tool. A technician contrives a purpose and then utilizes a tool as a means to achieving that purpose. And yet the possibilities for achieving the purpose are related to the character of the tool. A technician who wants to drive a screw ought not select a saw.

24. *Revolution*, 24-25.

25. *Revolution*, 11.

26. See his extended footnote in *Birth and Death*, 183-84.

27. *Structure*, 171.

28. *Birth and Death*, 22.

29. Becker used the example of baboon which is freer from "immediacy" through its ability to establish "second order" relations between itself and the stimulus object. The baboon is able to knock down a bunch of bananas with a stick.

30. Sally Kenel notes that Becker's obsession with debunking Freudian thought early in his career may have been a factor in his marginalization by the academy. *Mortal Gods: Ernest Becker and Fundamental Theology* (Lanham: University Press of America, 1988), 12. Becker himself acknowledged with regret the amount of energy he had spent on trying to refute Freud. Later in what he called his "mature work" he finally came to grips with what was "vital" in Freud. See the introduction to the second edition of *The Birth and Death of Meaning* (New York: Free Press, 1971). At this early stage, however, it is really Freud's pessimism about human nature that Becker is lashing out against—a pessimism that Becker felt was rooted in Freud's instinct theory. It is this he is trying to debunk.

31. *Structure*, 170.

32. *Structure*, 167.

33. *Structure*, 169.

34. This view of "openness" and "freedom from instincts" as defining the distinctively human seems to be characteristic of many contemporary approaches to human existence. Anthropologist Clifford Geertz claims that because "genetically programmed processes are so highly generalized in men" and "human behaviour is so loosely determined by intrinsic sources of information," humans get their cues to action from the symbol system in culture. "Religion as a Cultural System" in *The Interpretation of Cultures* (New York: Basic Books, 1973), 92-93. Sociologist Peter L. Berger is more radical when he says that

> *Homo sapiens* occupies a peculiar position in the animal kingdom.... Unlike the other higher mammals, who are born with an essentially completed organism, man is curiously "unfinished" at birth.... Man's world is imperfectly programmed by his own constitution. It is an open world. That is, it is a world that must be fashioned by man's own activity.... Only in such a world produced by himself can he locate himself and realize his life.... Biologically deprived of a man-world he constructs a "human" world. This world, of course, is culture. *The Sacred Canopy* (Garden City: Doubleday, 1967), 4-6.

This view is also represented in theology—for example in Wolfhart Pannenberg's dialogue with contemporary anthropology in his *What is Man?* (Philadelphia: Fortress Press, 1970). Pannenberg's first two chapters—which are entitled, "Openness to the World and Openness to God" and "Mastery of Existence Through Imagination," respectively—call to mind the themes dealt with in this work. Each of these views oppose "freedom" and "openness" to "nature" and "instinct." Each therefore reflects the Enlightenment view of a fundamental tension between humanity and the natural world that we identified in the introduction.

35. "Nature seems to have treated humans shabbily: only man arrives on the scene with no guiding instincts. Devoid of innate mechanisms by which to design a realm of experience, man had to carve out his own." *Revolution*, 11.

36. *Revolution*, 34.

37. Becker uses "self-feeling" and "self-esteem" as synonyms. The former term is, however, used generally with reference to organisms functioning on the pre-human level while the latter refers specifically to human organisms. See *Structure*, 157-58.

38. Becker likens the self or "ego" to a "control centre." *Birth and Death*, 2nd ed., 15.

39. For a good historical overview of the transition from a "given" world order which transcended (and grounded) human subjectivity to a view of order as created by the activity of the human subject, see Charles Taylor's *Sources of the Self: The Making of the Modern Identity* (Cambridge, MA: Harvard, 1989).

40. Becker, who liked to use examples from anthropological field work, cites the example of the Plains Indians who believed that their gods were stronger than the muskets of the white people. So strong was this belief that when they threw themselves into the line of fire of the guns it meant the "death of meaning" for them. *Birth and Death*, 2nd ed., 127-28. The gods were no longer in control. When modern "technological humans" sees the piling up of weapons and experiences the associated *anomie*—the realization of the potential destructive power of *their* gods—the precariousness of *that* vision is also highlighted.

41. The plural term "meanings" expresses Becker's point that while "meaning" is something all humans create, there is a plurality of meaning games played in different societies.

42. Becker uses different metaphors coupled with the term "meaning." For example, in *The Structure of Evil and Beyond Alienation* he uses the "game" metaphor ("meaning games," society as play form) following Johan Huizinga's *homo ludens*. (See, for instance, *Structure*, 212-18; *Beyond Alienation*, 142-43.) In his earlier works he uses a "drama" metaphor ("meaning-plots" and "meaning fictions"; see *Birth and Death*, 1st ed., ch. 8.) In order to include all these uses the rather bloodless term "meaning scheme" is employed here.

43. For a description of the same process of world construction from the perspective of sociology, see Berger, *Sacred Canopy*, chapters one and two. Berger calls the process where the meanings of society are merged with what that society takes to be the fundamental meanings of the universe "cosmization" (25f.). Like Becker, Berger sees the process of world construction as inherently precarious and fragile (29). At all times, the particular construal of the world by a society must "disguise" its constructed character by bestowing a necessary, ontological status on contingent, historical structures (33-36). Those who challenge, who offer a new way of seeing, who are innovators, are termed "deviants" (or even "mentally ill") and are relegated to the margins of that society—all for the sake of maintaining the fragile fiction (37). It is this process that Becker found so demeaning to the individual—which he saw as the cutting edge of the creative life process. The next section shall demonstrate why Becker thought individuals were forced into such a subservient role as legitimators and protectors of fictions. The end of this chapter shall see Becker trying to place the innovator over against cultural humanity.

44. See Ira Progoff's exposition of Adler's concept of "life style" in *The Death and Rebirth of Psychology* (New York: McGraw-Hill, 1956), 57-64.

45. See the next section.

46. *The Bonds of Love: Psychoanalysis, Feminism and the Problem of Domination* (New York: Pantheon, 1988), chapter four.

47. E. Becker, "Socialization, Command of Performance, and Mental Illness," *American Journal of Sociology* 67 (1962): 495.

48. Becker's formulation of culture as a scheme that has as its end the maintenance of self-esteem gives it a conservative role.

49. Garden City: Anchor Books, 1959.

50. "Socialization": 496. It is important to note well Becker's view of individuality as grounded in the ability to "keep others at a distance," and his view of sociality as the need to "use" others for self-affirmation.

51. "Socialization": 497.

52. "Socialization": 498.

53. On this see especially "The Second Great Step in Human Evolution," *Christian Century* 85:5 (Jan. 31, 1968), 135-39. Peter Berger identifies such "enslavement" as "alienation," which is

> ... an overextension of the process of objectivation, whereby the human ("living") objectivity of the social world is transformed in consciousness into the non-human ("dead") objectivity of nature. *Sacred Canopy*, 85-86.

54. See Progoff, *Death and Rebirth*, esp. 51-57.

55. Alasdair MacIntyre calls this kind of ethical view "emotivism." *After Virtue* (Notre Dame: University of Notre Dame Press: 1981), ch. 2 and 3.

56. "On Worldviews": 29.

57. *Birth and Death*, 158.

58. Philosopher Charles Taylor has chronicled the democratization of the aesthetic in his *Sources of the Self* (Cambridge: Harvard, 1990), 368-90. Taylor also calls this "expressivism."

59. Becker is inconsistent on the spelling of this crucial term, in some works spelling it "esthetics" and in others "aesthetics." Here the term is spelled the latter way. In quotations it remains whichever way Becker spells it in the text referred to.

60. *Structure*, 391. The tie-in between values, aesthetics and his ontology of striving is given in the title to chapter nine of *The Structure of Evil*, "Esthetics as Ethics: the Contribution of Descriptive Ontology."

61. *Structure*, 227. The emphasis is Becker's.

62. *Structure*, 213. "Neutral" in this context means "undirected." Humans are therefore "agents for" nature, directing it according to their creative energies.

63. *Structure*, 280. Becker says that this is "the moral of (Goethe's) *Faust.*" The reference is interesting because before Goethe retold the story of Faust, the Faust story was a tragic tale.

64. *Structure*, 390. "Man looks to nature as a guide to *his own creation of value.*" Emphasis is Becker's.

65. See the characterization of modernity in the Introduction above.

66. *Structure*, 213. It is unclear why Becker inserts the term "sparingly."

67. *Structure*, 177.

68. The term "social phenomenology" is from Joseph Scimecca, "Cultural Hero Systems and Religious Beliefs: The Ideal-Real Social Science of Ernest Becker," *Review of Religious Research* 21:1 (Fall, 1979): 62.

69. In fact nowhere does Becker talk about how any people in today's world are trained in ways that make them strong. Strength is a normative, rather than a descriptive concept, belonging to Becker's ideal individual. This does make sense, though, if understood to mean that only with a normative idea of the strong does the concept "weak" have critical power.

70. Becker doesn't suggest a simple causal relation between action and self-esteem. Stretching his economic metaphor it could be said that for Becker, one must have some capital (self-esteem) to invest (in objects). The return is dependent on the original investment, which is then reinvested again.

71. The phrase is found in *Beyond Alienation*, 181. This critique, based on his ontology of striving, has the following logic: People are stimulated to action by media hype, creating an artificial hunger (deficit, disequilibrium). But action is merely a transaction involving dollar symbols. Satisfaction is attained through possession, only to be disturbed again by further hype about "the new improved version." And so, "Life goes on," to quote the pop sage John Cougar Mellencamp, "long after the thrill of living is gone."

72. *Structure*, 255.

73. *Structure*, 256.

74. *Structure*, 285.

75. *Structure*, 284.

76. *Beyond Alienation*, 262.

77. *Beyond Alienation*, 261.

78. *Beyond Alienation*, 259.

79. Again Becker's language is somewhat lacking in precision. He speaks of "whole" objects, "fuller" objects, and "subjectivity" to refer to the same thing: the person considered as irreducible to a social role, the individual self as "greater than" the social self.

80. See *Birth and Death*, 194.

81. Bellah et al. call this kind of view "ontological individualism." This is " ... a belief that the individual has a primary reality whereas society is a second-order, derived or artificial construct...." *Habits of the Heart: Individualism and Commitment in American Life* (Berkeley: University of California Press, 1985), 334.

82. Becker does talk about different "levels" of meaning such as "individual" and "social" in *Structure*, 268. However these are spoken of in terms of the experience of the self and the sources of power for his activities. While Becker never explicates how these are to be related, it is helpful to see them in terms of his view of the life process as struggling between freedom and autonomy (the individual) and determinism (the social). Understanding this dialectic would answer the objection raised by Phillip Bosserman in his review of *The Structure of Evil*—that Becker fails to give the principle which connects the individual and the society. *American Sociological Review*, 35 (1970): 122.

83. The term is explored in *Structure*, 128-34.

84. *Structure*, 213.

85. That Becker actually had an ambivalent attitude toward sociality and the obligations entailed by life in society is indicated in a letter to Harvey Bates. Mourning his own lack of social involvement, he writes, "Didn't (Daniel) Berrigan say that if you were married you were sorely crippled as a free agent?!" Harvey Bates, "Letters from Ernest," *The Christian Century*, 94:8 (9 March, 1977): 226. That such a commitment as marriage is seen in such restrictive terms speaks of an either/or—similar in some ways to that set up by Soren Kierkegaard. It seems that Becker, like Kierkegaard, longed to be "The Single One." It is interesting to read Martin Buber's "The Question to The Single One" in *The Writings of Martin Buber*, ed. Will Herberg (New York: Meridian Books, 1956), 63-88. Comparing him to other Christian "solitary" thinkers, Buber writes of Kierkegaard,

> It is not irrelevant that beside Augustine stood a mother, and beside Pascal a sister ... whereas the central event of Kierkegaard's life was the renunciation of Regina Olsen as representing woman and the world (63).

Buber's criticism of Kierkegaard's essentialist view of the self (which claims relationality as secondary to the primary ontological reality of the individual) also holds for Becker.

86. *Capitalism and Progress*, translated by Josina Van Nuis Zylstra (Toronto and Grand Rapids: Wedge and Eerdmans, 1979), 10.

87. For the Hegelian master-slave image as I use it I am indebted to Jessica Benjamin (*Bonds*), and for the gift-call image to James Olthuis. Olthuis does not present it normatively as a dialectic, however. The use of the terms here is really a variation: modernity, in its insatiable quest to "liberate" the individual, forces us to choose between one or the other. In Olthuis' scheme, the self is simultaneously gift and call, *gaube* and *aufgabe*.

88. *Bonds*, chapter 2.

89. Catherine Keller's documentation of the way that the (modern male) separative self is placed over against the (modern female) soluble self is worth noting. *From A Broken Web* (Boston: Beacon Press, 1986), chapter 1.

90. In the middle of a blur of citations in *Beyond Alienation*, 213, Becker uses the term "gift." But the *way* it is used actually underscores the point here. First, humanity must "convert" life from a burden to a gift (note the dichotomy) " ... by consecrating it to the service of a self-transcending cause." The movement remains from burden to gift. Second, meaning remains something "given by" humanity to life. Third, the burden that Becker places on the shoulders of modern humanity is a terrible one: "to keep the universe going and evolving" (210). If "It is only in this way that life becomes a gift" (213), then we may be forgiven for refusing to shoulder the burden!

91. Perhaps the reader is wondering what exactly Becker could mean by "alienation." Alienation is "exile from the free and responsible aegis over one's own initiatory powers." *Structure*, 284. Therefore what Becker means as "alienation" is the opposite of "agency." As a concept,

> It holds up to man the bind in which the forms of society imprison his free human energies.... It is the guardian of sacred subjectivity in a mechanical and objective world. *Beyond Alienation*, 105.

92. See his "From System to Story," in *Truthfulness and Tragedy* (University of Notre Dame Press, 1977), 23-24.

93. Lifton, *Boundaries* (New York: Vintage Books, 1969), 44, cited by Hauerwas, *Truthfulness*, 62. In the quotation, Lifton goes on to say, "I want to stress that this protean style is by no means pathological as such, and in fact may be one of the functional patterns necessary to life in our times." See also Lifton's more recent book, *The Protean Self: Human Resilience in an Age of Fragmentation* (New York: Basic Books, 1993).

94. For one example of this confusion, compare the following quotations from *Structure*, 180 and 181 respectively. The emphasis is added: 1. *"We are all fetishists* by the nature of the problem." 2. "At any time when we have difficulty in making our energies felt, in making our environmental field come alive for our responses, *we tend to resort to fetishism...."*

95. The "normalization of brokenness" forms a thread of continuity in Becker's corpus, a thread which, as will be seen in the next chapter, spins out into a tragic view of humanity.

96. Take for example the following two quotations from *Beyond Alienation*, 145 and 155 respectively: 1. "Evil is banal, because evil is merely the toll of the *game* of society, and not of any basic *iniquity* in man." 2. "Evil is a result of man's disbelief in his right to his own independent and unique powers." The first of these quotations was in the context of a discussion of Hitler's Germany. If the difference between the social creation of meaning in the Third Reich and that anywhere else in the world is simply a matter of degree rather than kind, then it is understandable why Becker sets the individual over and against the society. But things are not that black and white (humanity is good and society is evil), as Becker would later be forced to recognize, thankfully. ("Or else one would have to wonder just what kind of creatures these 'humans' are ... that can so willingly participate in such slaughters"). The next chapter notes the way Becker confronted the dark side of humanity that he slighted here. However it shall also note that even there Becker gives no reason to condemn the Hitlers of this world.

As for the second quotation: those "men" who have come to believe in their independent powers have found rather unique and novel ways of poisoning the earth they have set those powers against.

97. *Structure*, 226.

98. *Structure*, 227.

99. *Structure*, 301.

100. *Structure*, 252.

101. *Structure*, 252.

102. See *Revolution*, 241-48.

103. *Structure*, 268. See also 244, where he writes, "The human animal attains dignity only when he subsumes the mechanical processes of nature to some higher, self-transcending ideal, one in which others can join." And what is this purpose? In

Beyond Alienation (chapter eight) Becker spells it out: nothing other than the freedom made possible by "potential command of nature and ... self critical knowledge" (220-21).

3. Tragedy and Heroism: Homo Heroica

The Birth of Tragedy

The Change in Tone in Becker's Later Works

The later works[1] of Ernest Becker display a marked change in spirit. Becker himself recognized that he had changed, saying in 1974 that he had "misgivings" about his earlier writings.[2] These misgivings involved an awareness that he had, in the 1960s, been too optimistic in conceiving the earth as "the stage for the future apotheosis of man."[3] Looking back on his career he admits that he had "been fighting against admitting the dark side of human nature for the last dozen years."[4] In the 1970s he takes "a less rosy view of human nature."[5] This picture is, in Becker's language, "starkly empirical,"[6] "irrespective of what we need or want,"[7] and yet "truly rounded."[8] Although it is pessimistic, it is not, at least as Becker sees it, cynical.[9] Perhaps it might be characterized as "tragic."[10]

Becker's writings, taken as a whole, reflect the struggles of an Enlightenment man. Although he himself saw his later thought as simply an extension of the "logical imperatives" of his earlier thought,[11] it is apparent that his later works are also works of self-critique. In his "first mature work,"[12] Becker writes:

> When one lives in the liberation atmosphere of Berkeley, California,... one is living in a hothouse atmosphere that shuts out the reality of the rest of this world.... The empirical facts of the world will not fade away because one has analyzed his Oedipus complex, as Freud well knew, or because one can now make love with tenderness, as many now believe. Forget it.... Men are doomed to live in an overwhelmingly tragic and demonic world.[13]

Who had lived and worked in the "hothouse atmosphere" of Berkeley but Ernest Becker, the one whose lectures on anthropology packed in almost 800 students? And who opposed "awareness" to "the empirical facts of the world" but Ernest

Becker, who had noted in 1967 that the goal of education was "seeing through" one's Oedipal complex? Who indeed was the one who now said that humanity was "doomed" but Ernest Becker, who earlier had claimed that Freud's pessimism disqualified him from inclusion in the hero roster of the "science of man"?

It was the same person who said that the great challenge of humanity was to push itself beyond enslavement to symbolic reinstinctivization toward the openness that was its heritage in creation who now said that,

> (Man) really can't evolve any further, that anything he might achieve can only be achieved from the real nightmare of his loneliness in creation and from the energies that he now has.[14]

How does Becker arrive at this point? After noting more carefully the change in tenor and language in his descriptions, three central features of Becker's change will be examined. First, a shift from a "nurture" to a "nature" view of human failings led to conceiving human existence in terms of an ontological paradox. Second, this brought about a change in Becker's anthropology from what shall be described as "monism" to a "dualism." Third, this brought about alterations in Becker's view of culture. Specifically the abandonment of his naive Rousseauean view that "man is good but society renders him evil" shall be noted.

Homo Heroica: The New Image of Humanity

Becker's earlier work raised the question of what humans are striving after. His answer was given in the phrase "firm meaning." The ideal image of Becker's science was termed by him *homo poeta*. *Homo poeta* is an individual, supported by society, striving to recreate the world after his or her own image. Such an individual achieved what Becker termed "satisfying mergers," "the weaving of spirit into matter," an experience of his or her own powers and the heightening of self-esteem.

Becker renames *homo poeta* as *homo heroica*. Despite the fact that the term "denial of death" has become associated with Becker, the real message of that book, as revealed by the section headings,[15] is about heroism. The *Denial of Death* continued Becker's synthetic effort to bring the disparate insights from a number of disciplines together under a unifying concept:

> I have written this book fundamentally as a study in harmonization of the Babel of views on man and on the human condition, in the belief that the time is ripe for a synthesis that covers the best thought in many fields....[16]

And in the introduction, Becker goes on:

One way of looking at the whole development of social science since Marx and of psychology since Freud is that it represents a massive detailing and clarification of the problem of human heroism.[17]

This clarification is the property not only of empirical science, but also of philosophy[18] and religion.[19] Its supposed universality is expressed in Becker's assertions that heroism can be studied as what humans are after and that heroism is what lies behind all religion and culture.

Becker's hero is the consummate individual. In fact the force that prevents us from really recognizing our urge to heroism is society. Society makes us shrink from admitting our heroic urge precisely because the hero as individual challenges the sameness of social order. Definite parallels are present here to what Becker wrote in *The Structure of Evil*: just as in that work, Becker said that societies grow as they feed off the creative energies of their citizens, so later in the *Denial of Death* he sees societies as feeding off the heroic urge of their citizens.

It is apparent that Becker's later work maintains a formal similarity to his earlier work in its organizing principle and universal scope. It is encyclopedic in the sense that it looks for global conceptual generalizations, under the auspices of "science," underneath particular situations. In this way it remains a strong expression of Enlightenment vision.[20]

The Underside of Humanity

The idea that there is a negative side to striving is not new for Becker. What *is* new is Becker's view that this downside is in the nature of human activity, rather than a result of failure. In his earlier work, he claimed that if persons were not able adequately to harmonize symbol and thing, they could compromise the evolutionary process. The downside then was the seductive power of the symbol to take the place of "reality."[21] Any disadvantage humans may have is not due to native "urges" or instincts. If there is evil in the world, it is due to "bad aesthetics," not a result of any native bent within humans.

Such innate urges were unacceptable to Becker in his earlier work because they compromised the idea of control, making humans the object of superordinate forces. However, in *The Denial of Death*, Becker claims that there is an inherent awareness in humans that they do *not* control their lives. This awareness of mortality—that one day, despite all efforts to put it off, they will die, is innate.[22]

Hence all heroism is a courageous attempt to defy mortality. The underside to heroism is expressed in terms of "the denial of death." As a consequence, human existence is now no longer interpreted under metaphors of control, but ones of "fate." Heroism is always "in spite of" ontological limitation.

Developmental and Structural Features of Homo Heroica

In his later work, Becker describes his image of humanity as *homo heroica* both structurally and genetically, (or developmentally). Characteristically he fails to distinguish the two. In the exposition of his later works I shall treat these different angles of approach to *homo heroica* separately. This treatment starts by considering developmental issues, taking note of the general terms that Becker uses in his descriptions. It then considers structural issues, taking note of the ontological paradoxes that *homo heroica* is caught up in. The outcome of this exposition will be the presentation of Becker's later view of humanity as a tragic figure.

The Underside of Human Development

Underlying Becker's view of heroism are four major ideas. They are 1) primary narcissism, 2) fear of death, 3) repression and 4) the *causa sui* project.

Primary Narcissism

The myth of Narcissus, the tragic hero who, upon seeing his own reflection in a pool, fell in love with it and eventually died because it was beyond his touch, has captivated many contemporary psychological thinkers. Becker felt that Erich Fromm's view, in particular, had special interpretive power for human existence. In narcissism he saw,

... the exposure of man's utter self-centredness and self-preoccupation, each person's feeling that he is *the one* in creation, that his life represents all life, and apotheosizes it.[23]

And so "each of us repeats the tragedy of the mythical Greek Narcissus: we are hopelessly absorbed with ourselves."[24] This "hopeless absorption" is rooted in the fact, for Becker, that in our deepest being we feel ourselves to be immortal. Thus narcissism is also the root of the denial of death principle.

The idea of narcissism is related to Becker's earlier idea of the primacy of self-esteem in human development. However, when Becker speaks of narcissism, he couples it with phrases like "omnipotence" and "limitless self-extension."[25] The original human experience is that of an undifferentiated self with a feeling of god-likeness.

But it does not take long before the "god" falls to earth. As the child grows and becomes aware of its manipulatory powers, it also becomes aware of its limits. It learns that it is "dragging around" a body, a body that is not amenable to control.

The child also learns that it is no longer a "magician" that can magically control its world through the mother. Its powers have limits.

The Denial of Death

The first paragraph of *The Denial of Death* reads,

> The idea of death, the fear of it, haunts the human animal like nothing else; it is a mainspring of human activity—activity designed largely to avoid the fatality of death, to overcome it by denying in some way that it is the final destiny for man.[26]

The fear of death is a universal. No individual, no culture, regardless of age, location or history is exempt from it. The fear of death is part of the structure of human existence. And yet Becker makes this claim alongside the concession that children, according to empirical research, don't know that their own death is inevitable until about the age of eight or nine.[27] For Becker this does not mean that the fear of death is "programmed into" the child, such that changing the program could do away with it. This is a radical step for one who had claimed in *The Structure of Evil* that a design for a renewed humanity started with changing the way children are educated and raised.[28] Becker now opposes such a "nurture" argument in favour of his "nature" argument.[29] Claiming that the fear of death is universal and "natural" raises two special problems for Becker. The first is the accounting for it in the experience of developing children. The second is accounting for it in the experience of adults—even well-adjusted ones. The second problem will be dealt with in the next subsection.

Becker answers the first problem by claiming that the fear of death is "a complex symbol."[30] As a complex symbol, it takes different forms at the various stages of human development. Originally it refers to the anxiety of object loss—something described briefly in chapter one as the driving force behind the development of the person as "controller." In *The Denial of Death* Becker extends this basic idea in a description of the infant's experience of its own powers.

In the state of primary narcissism, the omnipotent infant magically controls its environment by expressing a wish through crying. Mother comes immediately and satisfies the wish. But there comes a time when the infant's wishes are not fulfilled and it becomes aware of the limits of its powers. Unable to understand power relations, to understand why the fulfilment of its wishes is now arbitrary, the infant perceives the world as a threat. It loses a sense of control. The world becomes confusing. Mother becomes ambiguous.[31] The fear of death is not simply an awareness of the inevitability of a demise into the grave. "The grave" is but one symbolic form of a deeper malaise: the loss of the individual's powers over the world, the experience of threat, the fall from Eden, the expulsion from paradise. The hero is sometimes one who can cheat the inevitability of death by embracing it, gaining significance in its face, and therefore proving not to be subject to it.

Becker claims that humans do not simply fear death, but death with insignificance.[32] Indeed there are many examples of heroes who have sacrificed themselves for others and have gained notoriety for it. Their death was a death with heroic significance. And there are others who die for the sake of a cause. Nevertheless it is this urge to live on past one's (apparently) insignificant physical existence that is the primary impulsion for such activities.

Repression

Becker thinks that "human pretensions" include all human phenomena. And Becker's use of this term is telling: a "pretence" is a deception. To be "pretentious" is to "pretend" to be something one is not. All human phenomena, then, are attempts to "mask" the inner malaise.

A fair question here would be: "Don't we see 'well-adjusted' adults in the world?" Becker answers by saying that the "well-adjusted" person we admire so much is nothing more than a better liar than others. Such a person has learned to "repress" their basic fear, to call it something else.

The term "repression" is new to Becker's mature work. It is not unrelated to what Becker termed "abstraction" in his 1964 work *The Revolution in Psychiatry*. In chapter one of that work, as on page 50 of *Denial of Death*, Becker noted that the human person comes into the world "instinct free" but is continually bombarded by sensory stimuli. What Becker in 1964 called "abstraction" and in 1973 called "repression" is the learned "selection" of what stimuli the person is going to act in response to.

In his earlier work, Becker saw that humans have to act on the world in order to live. To fail to act in a satisfying way was to experience duality, a self alienated from the organic world. In *The Denial of Death*, Becker restates this idea as narcissistic vitality acting in order to "cover over" consciousness of mortality. We cannot live in the ambiguous and confusing world of the fallen child. We develop "character," a "vital lie," a self-deception that assures us that we are after all "in control."

Thus is the consciousness of our own weakness—our own contingency, our mortality—masked. Through repression we build up defenses, "character armour," to cover our vulnerability. All human activity is the outworking of this lie. Conversely, unless we learn to lie, there is no human activity at all. And yet through all this celebration of our illusory strength, the procrustean bed of denial remains. And so the later Becker actually deconstructs the earlier Becker, writing graffiti on his "Structure of Evil." Cheat our sense of impotence and bring in our "New [pretentious] Athenian Celebration of Man," yes. But remember, says Becker, "the skull always smiles at the banquet."[33]

The Causa Sui Project

Becker's earlier work saw "the Oedipal transition," reinterpreted by Alfred Adler, as the key to understanding the emergence of a symbolic animal, that is, an animal who earns self-esteem from symbolic performance. Becker continues this idea, but gives it a more radical edge in *The Denial of Death*, claiming that the fundamental question that the emerging child is asking is: "Will I become a free centre or a plaything of fate?"[34]

The Oedipal project is the overcoming of the bind on action through narcissistic inflation. Following Norman O. Brown, Becker puts forth the essence of the Oedipal project as becoming, "in Spinoza's words, *causa sui*—god."[35] There is no megalomania implied here; since the person must always maintain a sense of mastery in action, the best way to get out of the bind is for the child to think itself into the position of being a god.

Hence the Oedipal project is the project of becoming one's own father. It is the flight from "contingency," "passivity," "vulnerability." As we develop we realize we can no longer control the world by controlling mother. In Becker's terms, "The child wants to conquer death by becoming the father of himself, the creator and sustainer of his own life." The child wants to overcome its difficulty by becoming "... absolute controller of his own destiny."[36]

It's the law of the jungle: "Eat or be eaten." Or, in terms of our discussion, "control or be controlled." To assert control means however "escaping" the clutches of mother. The nurturing mother appears to the child as embodying in herself the "contingency," "passivity" and "vulnerability" that it is trying to escape from. Her mysterious connection to nature—in her bodily processes, in her menstrual cycles, in the life-giving substance that comes from her breasts—exudes "determinism." The child is repulsed by such natural determinism and tries to set itself over against it.[37]

The father, on the other hand, seems detached from nature. He is not subject to the same limitations that the mother is. In Becker's terms, he appears more "symbolically free" by virtue of his detachment. The father represents the social world outside the family "with its organized triumph over nature."[38] Thus the flight from mother is the flight to father. Opting for father means for Becker the attempt to model one's *causa sui* after the symbolic detachment from nature that the father represents.

"Individuality Within Finitude": A Shift in the Structure of Becker's theory

This new view of human development, of the dynamics of narcissism, fear of death, the Oedipal project and repression, is founded on a new view of the structure of human existence as dual. What is this structure?

The Transition from Monism to Dualism

Becker's later view of human development is that of a god fallen to earth. It is expressed developmentally in the *causa sui* project,[39] poetically in the phrase "gods with anuses," and structurally in a shift from monism to dualism. The earlier structure of Becker's theory may be described as a dialectical monism wherein objects bring the self into contact with the world and overcome alienation between the two poles in a satisfying merger called "the aesthetic." The aesthetic is a term describing the weaving of symbols into the world from which they are abstracted, through action. As the self experiences the "re-sounding" of the world, it also experiences the symbol as the real.

More specifically, the union of intention (mind) and action (world) in the aesthetic object is the only "real" humans can know. Humans "know," therefore, by exerting control over their environment. In this earlier view, the urge to merger with the world is a single ontological motive uniting the phenomenological realms of self and body. To experience these realms as separate is "abnormal" in terms of Becker's ontology and is a consequence of "poor funding," "shallow meanings" and "weakness."

But as demonstrated in the previous section of this chapter, Becker now sees a basic human motive in "life" and "death" denial. No longer do we strive after the "composition" of the real in aesthetic mergers, but the repression of the real for the sake of a narcissistic individual. The "denial of death" is the repression of creature consciousness by the only animal in nature aware of its mortality.

We are creatures. As creatures, we are subject to the same fate as all other creatures: death. Since Becker places words that echo "finitude" alongside the word "creatureliness," finitude becomes the defining characteristic of what it means to be a creature. Finitude defines our ultimate, creaturely limits.[40]

Transcendence, for Becker, means attaining uniqueness; differentiating the self from all others. Transcendence is the opposite of finitude because it is a transcendence of limitations which all creatures share *qua* creatures by the assertion of uniqueness on the part of the individual. With transcendence goes self-consciousness and individuality. Becker's shorthand term for the characteristically human structure is "*individuality within finitude*, self-consciousness and emergence from nature, yet boundedness to nature and death."[41] Note well the dualities in the following reference:

> This is the paradox: he is out of nature and hopelessly in it; he is dual, up in the stars and yet housed in a heart-pumping, breath-gasping body that once belonged to a fish and still carries the gill marks to prove it.... Man is literally split in two.... He has a symbolic identity that brings him sharply out of nature.

He is a symbolic self, a creature with a name, a life history.... Yet at the same time ... he is a worm and food for worms.[42]

But duality does not simply equal dualism.[43] Becker's earlier theory saw dualities within a single striving life process. These dualities were the poles that kept the one process unfolding. Now, Becker sets dualities in opposition. No merger, where the world "resounds" to the activity of the self, is possible. Finitude and transcendence, boundedness and boundless horizon, are inherent in the structure of human existence, and yet are paradoxical, irreconcilable opposites. This is why Becker's later theory is termed "dualist."

Body and Soul
"Man is an animal. Whatever else he is is built on top of this."[44] Becker makes this statement for two reasons: the first is its shock value. We are not used to thinking of ourselves as "animals." Our animality is the thing we most naturally deny. Second, the statement indicates that for Becker "significance" or "meaning" is something not given in nature, in animality. Rather it is constructed.

Since "nature" has not given a preset "role" for the body, humans must assign significance to it, usually in "contingencies" such as race/colour, age and sex. The arbitrariness of these as assigned roles is exhibited in cultural diversity. For example,

> The designation "old man" in one culture may entitle the actor to enjoy finally the power over others he has waited a lifetime to enjoy. The same designation in another culture may entitle the holder to be left out in the bush for the hyenas to carry off.[45]

If cultural constructions exhibit such relativity, then Becker claims they cannot be "real." Reality lies beneath cultural constructions. Meaning is purchased, Becker concludes, at the price of repressing creaturely existence. This is an important move away from a view of meaning as the weaving of human fictions into a responding world, since it indicates that meaning is no longer found in connection or integration, but in distinction and differentiation.

The phenomenological fact of our animality tells us only that we are "like" the other animals. We are born, we press other organisms down our gullet and excrete their remains, and we die. This we cannot accept because the *causa sui* tells us that we are unique and immortal. Becker sets individuality and difference over and against sameness. "Freedom" belongs to the realm of the individual, the self; while "nature" belongs to that of the body.

"Dualism" has often been used as a charge against Becker. But it is important that it be carefully qualified. Becker's dualism is not Cartesian or Manichean.[46] He does not want to privilege the self or soul over against the body. A Cartesian or Manichean dualism implies that "true" humanity consists in the distinctive, non-bodily "organs" of mind or spirit. For Becker, paradox is what makes us human, not any particular "organ." Salvation cannot be found in a disembodied existence, since this would no longer be a "human" existence. It is within the interstices of paradox that humanity is located. Both self and body must be held together, in a "balance."[47]

Twin Ontological Motives

In Becker's earlier theory, the basic human motive was singular, explained around the terms "self-esteem maintenance," "firm meaning" and "aesthetic experience." When Becker embraced the ontological paradox of individuality within finitude he was led to assert that each phenomenological realm is driven by an "ontological motive." In a dual structured animal, each level has its own way of realizing the quest for satisfaction.[48]

Humans are driven by this ontological paradox in two contradictory directions. In one, the drive is to individuation and uniqueness. The name for the ontological motive that Becker assigns here is *eros*. *Eros* describes that feeling of specialness gained by working one's special gift on the world. It refers to the urge to shine and to stick out.[49]

This drive is opposed by another. This is the drive to identification, to unification with other life forms, the "natural" organismic urge to "at-one-ness" with the cosmic process. This motive Becker calls *agape*. *Agape* speaks of yielding to the other, a self-giving suspension of the *causa sui* project.[50] It denotes the need to belong, to reach out for the other. It also refers to the need to identify with some self-transcending cause.[51]

It is apparent that both of these motives are equal in force because Becker doesn't see redemption in terms of suppressing one principle by means of the other. And so the result is a tragic paradox which admits of no resolution:

> Man wants the impossible: he wants to lose his isolation and keep it at the same time. He can't stand the sense of separateness, and yet he can't allow the complete suffocating of his vitality.[52]

If one motive is not negated by the other, then some means of balancing the two must come along. This "means" is culture. But first something Becker calls creature guilt must be discussed, for it is this guilt that makes balancing the motives necessary.

The Double Bind of Guilt

There is a price to pay both for uniqueness and for identification. People are victimized by both drives. Guilt comes both from individuation and identification.[53] It is not simply the violation of some moral code, nor a reification of subjective shame. It cannot be resolved simply through "awareness" of one's early "twisting."[54] Guilt is the inescapable result of the human paradox.

Sticking out from nature, "detaching oneself from the background of things," brings guilt. This guilt is "the guilt of being."[55] It comes with self-consciousness. Individuation means "sticking out from nature." The more we stick out, the more self-conscious we feel and the more we need to either repress the guilt and "move on" or appeal to fellow creatures to tell us "it's okay" to be a self, to stick out, to be different. We are, as it were, "damned if we do and damned if we don't." In appealing to our fellow creatures, we show our dependence on others. If we cannot, we "bog down" and lose the ability to act.[56]

The *agape* motive also creates guilt. Identification with others and occupation with the everyday cultural world weighs on the individual. Not individuating is experienced as a failure to fulfil the *causa sui* project. To identify is to stand against the whole humanization process, as Becker describes it.

Becker's view of guilt is that of a "bind" on action. More specifically, the bind is a paralysing "double bind." It is the experience of "fear and powerlessness."[57] How is it expiated?

Expiation has to take place from the "outside," from a source of power that leaves the individual "in awe." The dynamic of expiation begins, for Becker, in the relationship with the parents. The affirmation of the *causa sui* project of the child is derived from the parents who single out the child as locus of primary value. This is called *transference* and is a function of power. Power is the most important factor in human development for Becker. Awed by power, the person feels that their individuality is part of a larger scheme of transcendence which can both expiate existential guilt and guarantee a secure place for action in the world. And as Becker also says, power is precisely power to deny creatureliness, mortality.

Conclusion: Tragic Humanity

Man is literally split in two: he has an awareness of his own splendid uniqueness in that he sticks out of nature with a towering majesty, and yet he goes back into the ground a few feet in order to blindly and dumbly rot and disappear forever.[58]

Becker's later thought has been considered under the headings of "genesis" and "ontological structure." Each of these has shown a shift in Becker's thought toward a vision of human existence as bound by paradox. Self-consciousness means thinking of ourselves as gods. But nature has shortchanged us by giving us limitless aspirations in a limited world. Hence we are bound to fail in our quest to be *causa sui*.

Becker's dominant metaphor in this phase of his thought, that of the hero, is wholly appropriate for his vision. Volney Gay has noted that the hero, in classical thought, exists in a middle realm between the natural and the supernatural.[59] Neither fully god nor fully creature, the hero is in Becker's terms "a god that shits."[60]

Neither animal nor angel, the heroic consciousness bears the brunt of ontological paradox:[61]

> (Man) was given a consciousness of his individuality and his part-divinity in creation, the beauty and uniqueness of his face and name. At the same time he was given the consciousness of the terror of the world and of his own death and decay. This paradox ... is the true "essence" of man....[62]

There is an interesting parallel between Becker's assertion that humanity is caught up in a structural ambiguity, of a "complete powerlessness to overcome that ambiguity, to be straightforwardly animal or angel," with the Greek tragic hero Prometheus:

> Prometheus, the European culture hero *par excellence*, is neither fully divine, since he and his fellow Titans are conquered by Zeus, nor fully human, since he does not perish on his rock of suffering.[63]

Taken as a whole, Becker's work with its early optimism and its later pessimism, displays the Enlightenment vision of the individual, with limitless possibility, brought radically "down to earth." Becker's use of Rousseau's maxim that "man is good but society renders him evil" changed radically. It is in humans as individuals, rather than in culture (society), that the ambiguity is located. Culture is now simply the outworking of paradox and the result of the need to balance the twin ontological motives. The dynamics of evil and society will now be examined.

The Dynamics of Culture

Becker's description of the human condition has been examined developmentally and structurally. The terrors of the world of the child, of being born into a fearful world, of recoiling from that world and yet being urged toward emergence as an individual, are grounded in an even more basic ontological problem.

It is impossible, in Becker's view, that humans can live in the world "as it is." While other animals fit into the world, inasmuch as they have been given instincts, we are fated not to fit into the world. Our primary reality is the world given in culture, a world which functions to deny the basic human situation through a creative illusion. Such an illusion serves to balance the twin ontological motives.

Transference

That which serves to balance the motives is the transference object. The initial response of the infant to the world is anxiety, and that anxiety is dealt with in repression. The transference object is the means to repressing the world. It is a falsification of the world,[64] a "rebellion against reality."[65] Since we cannot emerge as individuals in reference to the world, we do so in relation to another person. This other person becomes the focus for all our fears and hopes. The other is the one we yield to as a buffer against anxiety.

Transference is then a kind of fetishism. It is also spoken of by Becker as a kind of idolatry. Transference is literally "a transfer" of power to the other, of responsibility to the other. If all power, as mentioned above, is power to deny mortality, then transference is the gaining of immortality through yielding to an other.[66] Transference is rooted in the loss of control that is sensed by the infant. If we cannot control our environment, then our urge to control must be placed onto a narrow portion of the world. The transference object gives

> ... a certain degree of sharply defined individuality, a definite point of reference for (our) practice of goodness and all within a certain level of safety and control.[67]

Put another way, such an object grants "a *localized stimulus* that takes the place of the whole world."[68]

Chapter one questioned Becker concerning whether fetishism is necessary, or whether it is rather a learned behaviour. There is a similar problem here concerning transference. Transference is both an ontological necessity and a developmental phenomenon. The tragedy for Becker is not found in transference heroics itself, but rather in the quality of those heroics; that they are not under the control of the individual but are heroics the individual *uncritically* buys into.[69]

> But transference is *also* spoken of as a natural reflex: (Man) is forced to address his performance ... to his fellow creatures, as they form his most compelling and immediate environment, not in the physical or evolutionary sense in which like creatures huddle up to like, but more in the spiritual sense. Human beings are the only things that mediate meaning, which is to say that they give the only human meaning that we can know.[70]

Hence, "transference is a natural function of heroism, a necessary projection in order to stand life, death and oneself...." Transference is the means to avoid looking life full in the face. Transference, to use another image, is a description of the child hiding behind the skirt of mother. And yet we are all children at heart, afraid of the world "out there," taking refuge in our safe objects. This difficulty reappears when Becker's view of cosmic heroics, on God as an ideal object, is considered. For now the phenomenon of culture, which for Becker always refers to as "inauthentic" and "narrow" transference, needs examination.[71]

Culture and the Armoured Individual

Becker thought that culture provided a path for "safe" heroism (by which he meant a heroism that was "tolerable" within the culture);[72] for balancing the ontological motives by allowing limited individuation within a scheme that promised participation in the life of a community that outlived the individual.

This "balancing of the motives" doesn't get Becker's human out of its dualism, however. In fact culture replicates the same dualism that the individual experiences in his interactions with nature. In order to be affirmed, individuals have to give themselves over to the collective. Paradoxically, then, in order to get on with their drive to uniqueness, to be master over their own destiny, everyone needs to become dependent on something outside their individuality. Narcissism and identification, *eros* and *agape*, gaining the self (and losing the world) and losing the self (and gaining the world) are two sides of the same human coin.

All humans of necessity live out a lie. Since to see our real condition is "to die," we cannot function as humans without illusions. Personality, or "character," is another name for the lie we live, the name we receive by our assuming of a "fictional" cultural role. The self is an armoured self, shielded from the "real" paradox which is the true human condition.[73] For Becker, who came to this conclusion as early as 1969, such a view of the human personality was a great advance:

> I have arrived at a definition of the human personality that I think reflects the basic truth: that what we call man's personality or his life style is really a series of techniques that he has developed, and that these techniques have one major end in view — the denial of the fact that he has no control over death or over the meaning of his life.[74]

Giving up control, ... renouncing one's ego, is taken up into the play of individual versus culture. In order to repress the fact that we have no control, we allow others to control us. But in allowing others to control us, we are no longer "number one," no longer self-determining. Need for the other disallows freedom, in Becker's view. Resolving the human dilemma means becoming less than fully human, which for Becker means less of an individual.[75]

The Cultural Causa Sui

Cultures not only replicate the basic human duality, granting an illusory world in which persons actually *can* become heroes, but they also express their own *causa sui* project. Cultures are themselves impelled to stand over against other cultures. How?

"Reality" can only support one hero system, in Becker's view. However the social sciences have discovered great differences in the way hero systems are set up.

This knowledge is subversive, however: it can never become public because we dare not acknowledge that there might be another way to be a hero. We surrender to a cultural "way"—a surrender that, if done correctly, is absolute.[76]

Since an absolute relativises all other ways to itself, all "other" cultures are necessarily seen as deluded.[77] Not only deluded, but *degraded*. Becker used these formulations to explain all the bloodshed in human history. War[78] is not a matter of "right" versus "wrong," but rather a matter of competing immortality accounts where

> "Our nation" and its allies represent those who qualify for eternal survival; we are the "chosen people." ... All those who join together under one banner are alike and so qualify for the privilege of immortality; all those who are different and outside that banner are excluded from the blessing of eternity.[79]

War for Becker becomes a dramatization of one immortality ideology against another, and victory in war is "proof" that the gods favoured the winners. By killing the enemy we prove that the other is mortal. By degrading the enemy, the other is reduced to the status of an animal; just another creature.[80]

The dynamic of expiation is carried out here also. *This* expiation requires a projection of good versus evil: the task of a culture is to carry out a mission to stamp out evil, to cleanse the world of defilement.[81] As Becker put it in an interview,

> We each need a Jew or a nigger, someone to kick, to give us a feeling of specialness. We need an enemy to degrade, someone we can humiliate to raise us above the status of creatures.[82]

In other words, each culture creates its own "evil empire" that it gains identity over against. If people cannot derive meaning just from being creatures, if they cannot find a "natural" world to act in, they must reduce the world to something they *can* act upon. This then creates an artificial crisis, an enemy, as the locus of the creation-denying energies released.[83] This evil empire must be destroyed if the cultural *causa sui* project is to succeed. But the evil empire cannot be "entirely" destroyed, since that would threaten the project just as much.[84]

Perhaps Becker's point illustrates the boredom felt at the end of modernity, a problem previously noted as a symptom of the contemporary malaise. As Francis Fukuyama put it in his notorious essay "The End of History?"[85] the end of history, as a metaphysical triumph of good over evil, is a disappointment. The end of history is marked by "a VCR in every home," rather than a sense of world historical fulfilment. The "evil" Russian empire has collapsed.[86] Yet we find ourselves in a crisis of meaning. Where are our heroics to be directed? What else do we need to gain victory over? What darkness can we project our light against?

Prospects for Modernity

Fukuyama notwithstanding, in Becker's terms, the western "lie" is breaking down and there is nothing immediately present to replace it.[87] While this apocalyptic tone is not absent from his earlier work, it comes to its most profound expression in the 1970s. Looking back on his experience in the turbulent sixties, Becker saw the need for genuine heroism as a key unlocking the sense of alienation among the students he taught at Berkeley.[88] A lengthy passage from *Denial of Death* is worth quoting in full:

> The crisis of modern society is precisely that the youth no longer feel heroic in the plan for action that their culture has set up. They don't believe it is empirically true to the problems of their own lives and times. We are living a crisis of heroism that reaches into every aspect of our social life: the dropouts of university heroism, of business and career heroism, of political action heroism; the rise of anti-heroes, those who would be heroic each in his own way or like Charles Manson with his special "family," those whose tormented heroics lash out at the system that itself has ceased to represent agreed heroism.[89]

Indeed Becker's prophecy seems remarkably apt for so-called "Generation X," the children of the flower children. As the fabric holding society together breaks down, the ambiguity of its hero systems is exposed. Becker goes on to say:

> The great perplexity of our time, the churning of our age, is that the youth have sensed—for better or worse—a great social-historical truth: that just as there are useless self-sacrifices in unjust wars, so too there is an ignoble heroics of whole societies: it can be the viciously destructive heroics of Hitler's Germany or the plain debasing and silly heroics of the acquisition and display of consumer goods, the piling up of money and privileges that now characterizes whole ways of life, capitalist and Soviet.[90]

Hero systems, as the contemporary one has made plain, are ways in which "man makes of his freedom a prison."[91] But Enlightenment man that he is, Becker claims that a good look at the empirical "facts" of the world can grant moderns space to realize the dream of freedom by a new heroics. Despite his stunning critique of the failure of "human nature," Becker still affirms:

> There is nothing in man or nature that would prevent us from taking some control of our destiny and making the world a saner place for our children.[92]

While we can never overcome our paradoxical nature, nor defeat evil and death,[93] Becker says that at least we[94] are aware of our sickness. "We know," he is saying, "what it is that constricts us." Moreover we can still formulate a non-utopian vision, a way of coping with the darkness of human nature, a way of holding off the full unleashing of the destructive powers of humanity. This "vision in the night"[95] concerns "cosmic heroics," the projection of one's *causa sui* project onto the stars. And yet it remains a painful and tragic shot in the dark.

Impossible Paradox and the Closure of Human Possibility

The Inescapable Need for Illusion

Criticising the Critics

While Freud, the venerated father of psychoanalysis, wanted to see humans as striving toward the real, as progressively overcoming illusion in the attainment of some measure of "health," Becker, on the other hand, claims that the real, in the sense of a comprehensive picture of life-as-it-is, is precisely what is inaccessible to us. Earlier in his writings Becker had proposed that since "reality" is greater than we are, our knowing is always "in part." Our "realities," our attempts to create what is real through fictions, while expressing the great life force can never capture the power of the whole. To survey the whole we would need to stand outside it.[96]

In *The Denial of Death* Becker adds an even more profound reason why banishing illusion in favour of a sober, scientific view of "reality" is not possible. We can't tolerate the real, for reality debunks our pretensions to individuality and transcendence. Even sober scientist Sigmund Freud tried to overcome his own fear of mortality by psychoanalysis, which became his personal immortality scheme.[97]

The human paradox means the end of utopian dreaming. Psychoanalysis has come a long way since Freud, especially in terms of the role of death-fear in human development. Yet while Becker claims to have learned much from revisionist Freudians, he notes that they too have embraced a utopian view of human nature. Calling them "psychological religionists," Becker claims that they have posited repression as the evil that must be overcome, on the premise that health will come only if a way can be found to live an "unrepressed life."

Norman O. Brown especially is singled out by Becker on this point. It was Brown who recast many traditional Freudian categories into a form forged around the problem of the denial of death. Becker found these reformulations "brilliant," and made good use of them.[98] But Brown's conclusions were different from Becker's. For example, Brown claims that the abolition of repression would mean a new relation to the body and the abolition of death fear.[99]

Becker found Brown's "optimistic" picture rooted in a "nurture" perspective on repression. Repression is a result of environmental and developmental factors. By changing the nurturing environment and bringing in new ways of raising children, repression can be done away with. Becker has claimed, to the contrary, that the problem is not simply nurture, but nature. Nature compels humans to the *causa sui* project. The unique way that the child sees the world, as a nightmarish and threatening place, means that we must set ourselves over against it—find a way of bringing it under our control—or else risk the void.[100]

If the dreaming of revisionist Freudians like Norman Brown misses the mark for Becker, so does that of revisionist Marxists like Herbert Marcuse. Claiming that the fear of death is a function of ideologies of control, Marcuse envisioned an ideal society in which the fear of death is abolished through an elimination of the ideologies that support it.[101] Becker responds that the fear of death goes deeper than ideology, and repression of this fear is what brings about the miracle called "human nature."[102] Without repression there would not be any such thing as "human nature."

Becker's criticism of the heralds of the unrepressed life can be summarized in one phrase: human duality is immutable. There is no way, he says, that we could remain human without repression of our creatureliness. Duality is structurally basic to our peculiar nature. Transformation is impossible. Adaptation is the only way to survive. If we can only survive by lying about ourselves and the world, then we need the best lie possible.

Creative Illusion

By making the assertion that an illusion can be "non-destructive," Becker is saying that while humans are tragic animals condemned to live in perpetual tension, that tension need not lead to the destruction of human (and non human) life. While we cannot change our nature, we can, within the limits of that nature, change our relationship to the world. The keyword is therefore no longer *transformation*, but *adaptation*.

The question, for Becker, is never one of living "without illusions." Rather the question is, "Which illusions are life-affirming?" The term "life-affirming" has a negative and a positive side. Negatively it refers to "non-destructive." Becker claims that humans *can* turn all the energy and time and resources spent on destroying illusory "others" and turn them against "the real enemies" of hunger and oppression.[103]

Positively, an illusion must be "empirically real." This does not mean that an illusion must enable us to see nature "as it is," "red in tooth and claw." To see this would be to die. Rather, "empirically" real means for Becker the quality of an illusion that enables us to see *ourselves* as *we* really are: striving organisms on a quest for transcendence. Another way of putting this would be to say that Becker is calling not for a confrontation with raw reality without our armour, but rather for better armour with which to face the world.

The Limits of Science

But how is it that the same person who admits that we cannot tolerate the real can now, albeit formally, describe reality? And not only this, but he claims he can describe reality in such a way as to relativize all other ways of constructing reality. Is Becker asserting that his description of reality is not also "constructed?" What is going on here?

Enlightenment science, as Becker hears it, has told us that we were lying to ourselves when we thought our culture provided a set of timeless norms for all humans. Science has, in a word exposed the relativity of hero systems around the world. Science has a critical, iconoclastic function. Science tells us what is *not real*. But without a positive, real-istic vision that seeks to answer the question "What is and is not possible," utopian dreaming (everything is possible) can only get us into more trouble. Unfortunately, Becker tells us that very little is possible for the conflicted, paradoxical creature-god he calls humanity.

Becker has also criticized science as lending itself easily to the "anal sadistic" urge to overcome "nature" through manipulation and control.[104] Becker claims, with great urgency, that unless we bring our urge to dominate under the control of a life-affirming vision, the human race is doomed along with the rest of the planet.

There is reason, however, to question how internally consistent Becker is. In 1962 he had already berated the sadist for reducing the world, out of insecurity, to a single principle, for reducing cultural life to "simple" motives. If Becker really wants to tie the bent of western science to "anal sadism" then he needs to question whether his early reduction of all human striving to "self-esteem," or his later reduction to "immortality striving," does not also function sadistically. Indeed the glee with which Becker "rips off the mask" of our pretensions would seem to point to a "dark side" of Becker's own writing.

Modern humanism has indeed stripped the world of inherent meaning and has sadly failed in its efforts to restore meaning through creative construction. Modern humanism has also done away with the possibility of revelation by any means other than science. Science is the only authoritative bar of judgment. Now, as Becker sees it, science is only able to disclose limits, to show finitude, to relativize pretentious meaning-creation. The truth Becker tells us is that we cannot stand naked before the flux. Or, to invoke the biblical story (which Becker also invoked), our nakedness revealed makes us clutch for covering.[105] We need an illusion or else we die of exposure.

Drawing the Balance Sheet

This chapter has shown the core of Becker's later anthropology as his description of the essence of the human person as paradoxical. Humans are split between two realms, involving two ontological motives: the urge to heroic transcendence, to uniqueness and identity; and the urge to merger, to identification with a whole. Culture takes on the role of balancing these motives by granting a scheme for heroism on the one hand and by becoming identified with the "whole" on the other. Becker's critique of contemporary culture is its failure to provide a system or scheme by which these motives can be balanced. The present hero system has lost its legitimacy, and this has meant an enormous crisis for people. Finally, some of Becker's fellow social critics have been discussed, especially how they share Becker's broad diagnosis of the problem, and yet are censured by him for prescribing that which is impossible—changing human nature. On the contrary, Becker tells us, we can never change our basic structure of "twoness." We can only find more creative illusions that adequately balance the motives.

And so this discussion moves toward the sphere of the most creative illusion, the ideal balancing of the twin ontological motives:

> Can we imagine any kind of quietude and balance between the urge to cosmic heroism and the dribbling, pink orificed body of a primate life?[106]

Becker calls this kind of balance a "cosmic heroics."

Cosmic Heroics

A Creational Stage

> Man is an animal that has to do something about his ephemerality.... To be a hero means to leave something behind that heightens life and testifies to the worthwhileness of existence; ... the important question is *how* we are to be heroes.[107]

Becker's view of cultures as religions is that their "artificially fixed world," created in response to the basic "minus" of human existence, is too small; that its range of concerns is too narrow, its list of enemies too marginal. In the quotation above, Becker notes that the problem is not with heroics *per se*, but with the *kinds* of heroics extant in the world. After the secret of the relativity of hero systems is let out, the only satisfying heroism is a creational one.

Three features of such a heroism can be distilled from Becker's writings. First, a creational heroism would affirm the *causa sui* project as the task of "working one's own special gift on the world,"

... to fashion something (*eros* motive)— ... an object or ourselves—and drop it into the confusion (*agape* motive), make an offering of it, so to speak, to the life force.[108]

Becker's anthropology needs a way that the urge to individuate and the urge to identify can become complementary and reinforcing, rather than the cause of anxiety. Rather than conforming individuality to one "relative" narrowing down of the world, Becker's "ideal" individual would need (through cosmic heroism) to hold his or her individuality even on a stage as wide as the cosmos, and yet "make a contribution." As an affirmation of the *causa sui*, cosmic heroism would consecrate the individual life.

Second, such a heroism would not seek to escape the dilemmas of human existence, but face them. Earlier I have noted Becker's critique of the present system as empirically untrue. By "empirically true," then, an ideal hero system gives us the means to see our plight in a state of "relative unrepression." In other words, Becker is calling for an illusion that lets the most amount of "reality" in. Becker's ideal is not a transcendence *of* our limits, but rather an adaptation *to* those limits.

Third, the stage for such cosmic heroic activity is no longer the culturally relative stage of "immanent" hero systems, but rather the "creation" itself. Becker thought that this would get us beyond the destructive alternatives that pit race against race and society against society through the most powerful kind of relativizing: what is this society, this war, compared with the grandness of creation?

But to what, or to whom, is one's gift to be offered? What of the *agape* motive? Who is the affirming "other?" How is the guilt of being to be dealt with? Where will justification or expiation come from? It is here that Becker brings to the fore that word so fearful to the Enlightenment: God. The great religions of the world parallel cultures in functioning as hero systems. Cultural systems inevitably break down because they are based on a "partializing" idolatry. We need to be justified by something truly transcendent. Becker thought that beyond all contingent particularity there was "God."

A Religious Vision

It is not a trivial matter that Becker, rather than starting with religion and God, brings it in at the end of his works. His method is a kind of *via negativa*: exhaust the possibilities for whole humanness through the most rigorous and bold insights of science, then show how science fails to give us what we really need, then bring in the ideal: God.

Becker uses the term "religion" in at least two ways. First, he uses it in a general phenomenological sense to describe the ways that collectives repress "reality" by death denying schemes of transcendence. In this way societies (even atheistic ones) are "religious."[109] Second, he uses it as an alternative to culture, as a way of doing better what culture does: providing illusions to live by.

Culture as Religion

While the former view has much to commend it, Becker casts it in an overly negative light. Culture is a "covering" for our "natural" weakness. Becker speaks about culture[110] as a way of rendering the world so that the motives are balanced.[111] We are given a safe path for heroism, as well as a collective to which to refer ourselves. The former satisfies the *eros* motive, while the latter the *agape* motive.

Becker says that cultures are "religious"[112] because they offer transcendence schemes,[113] ways of balancing the motives, of being heroic.[114] They also provide something to yield to.[115] And, over against other cultures, they have ready made scapegoats to absolve guilt.

For Becker, culture is *de facto* already directed toward "getting away from" creation, repressing creatureliness. Becker equates "culture" with "idolatry." As long as we find our longings fulfilled in culture, we are "living in a world of idols."[116] As already discussed, culture is involved in the dynamic of human transference, "the universal distortion of reality by the artificial fixing of it."[117] The essence of this fixing is the effort "to make the world something other than what it is." Culture is a function of basic human insecurity. But culture-religion is doomed from the start. Becker is unyielding when he says that the finite cannot ground human urges to the infinite.

> In order to get (a centring in himself) man has to look beyond the "thou," beyond the consolations of others and of the things of this world.[118]

This phrasing, echoing similar expressions in *Beyond Alienation*,[119] shows that the issue here is *trust*. All humans entrust themselves to something. The dynamics of heroism and expiation of ontological guilt both entail a "letting go" in faith, an entrustment of the meaning of one's life to another. Since culture as Becker sees it can only fulfil this "other" role as a deception, it is inauthentic. Once the deception is unmasked, the person is left facing the void. Facing squarely the truth that finite creatures are doomed—that humanly constructed cultures grow, gain ascendency over others, then unravel and die—raises the question of where the *ultimate* grounding for heroism can be found.

Thus awareness of the inadequacy of one's trust in the things of this world is a springboard into a more authentic trust,

> ... as long as man is an ambiguous creature he can never banish anxiety; what he can do instead is to use anxiety as an eternal spring for growth into new dimensions of thought and trust. Faith poses a new life task....[120]

Here faith is seen not as a universal feature of all humans, but rather as a consequence of having seen through the deception of culture. Some, not all, have faith. For such people, a new life task is posed.

Religion as Alternative to Culture
    In the second sense, religion is used to describe an *alternative* to culture, as a better way to carry out what cultures are supposed to do. While the first use of religion refers to misdirected transcendence schemes, the second refers to an alternative transcendence scheme. While bearing affinities to the great religions of the world such as Christianity, Buddhism and Judaism, Becker insists that his ideal scheme is itself nameless. He dare not get too specific, too concrete, for fear of losing God's transcendence:

> Anything less than God is not rational (given the miracle of creation). Anything more than the abstraction "God" (i.e., possession of certain knowledge about the actual Creator and his plan) is not possible. We can't know ... ultimate reality since we ourselves are transcended by it.[121]

The "God" of Becker's ideal religion is defined as that which is opposite the idols of culture. Becker's God is abstract and independent, rather than concrete, near at hand and immanent. Any more specificity and God would be narrowed down to the creature level. God cannot be partialized, rendered or grasped as a real object.
    If by "certain knowledge of the actual Creator," Becker means knowledge of the same kind as that striven for by the sciences, then his point is hard to dispute. The kind of knowledge that moderns seek is knowledge that issues forth in control. If we could control our object, it would not be transcendent, and this would bring us to the void again.
    Such a God is the ideal and perfect "other" for humanity as imagined by Becker: No human relationship can bear the burden of godhood, and the attempt has to take its toll in some way on both parties. The reasons are not far to seek. The thing that makes God the perfect spiritual object is precisely that God is abstract—as Hegel saw. God is not a concrete individuality, and so does not limit our development by God's own personal will and needs.[122]
    We can seek but we can never find this God. As an abstract entity, Becker's God lacks the insecurity of the creature. Becker's God needs no absolution, no expiation. His God is self-absolving and wholly other.

> God's greatness and power is something we can nourish ourselves in, without its being compromised in any way by the happenings of this world. No human partner can offer this assurance because the partner is real.[123]

And yet Becker's non-specific God lacks a revealed character that would lead us to believe even in the possibility of divine absolution. In fact, from within Becker's definitions it is impossible to attribute *character*, whether essentially or analogically, to God. A separatist God has no reason to armour Godself. Moreover Becker's God, as abstract, is by definition non-revelatory.[124]

Problems with Becker's View

Three features of Becker's view seem especially problematic. First of all, Becker's description of the human paradox as individuality within finitude not only begs the question of an infinite (abstract) referent of authentic trust, but also serves to empty creatureliness of positive meaning content. Second, while Becker claims that science is completed by religion, at the end of the day his God actually is subject to science. Becker's God as non-revelatory discloses the continuity of his modernistic vision: science is revelation. Third, while Becker claims that all cultures are lies, he fails to account for the supposed "truth" of his own view. This is disclosed in some startling contradictions in his own use of the category "repression." Putting these together, Becker's God could be named as a quasi-deistic "God of the gaps."

Individuality Within Finitude

Jane Kopas has correctly understood Becker as defining the term "creatureliness" with the term "finitude."[125] Setting things up this way dooms creatureliness to be understood negatively, in terms of *limits*. Certainly for Becker, who once thought of human existence as limitless in possibility, as ever bringing the new into the world, the acknowledgement of existence as ontologically limited is negative. Unfortunately it also ignores that creatureliness must also be understood relationally: in relation to God (the creator) and to other creatures.[126] The "given" is understood fundamentally as limitation.

Kopas argues that the term "finitude" is non-relational and individualistic. Since Becker has asserted that the individual is the end of the life process, this actually fits quite well with his theoretical concerns. It also explains why Becker holds fast to an abstract view of God. If the revelation of ontological limitations is nothing more than the revelation of "finitude" (and by extension "infinitude"), then "certain knowledge of the actual creator and his plan" is indeed impossible. This turns out quite well for Becker, since he identifies individuation with making a "unique" contribution to life. If the individual "knew" of the plan of the creator, then he or she would have to conform any deed to that plan or else face the void again.[127] But there would remain another problem: that of autonomy. For a revealed God would place further limitations on the individual. A revealed God with a revealed plan would disallow the *eros* motive of individual creativity.

Rather than affirming what any of the extant religions of the world do for people, then, Becker is in fact offering an alternative religion to any that recognize a creator actively involved in and disclosed to creation. The category "finitude" actually protects Becker from the incursion of any God who might come alongside us. Rather, we must reach toward God. It is in our hands.[128]

Science and Religion, or the Religion of Science?

For Becker it is science that discloses our ontological paradox. Science has disclosed the basic ontological structure of existence as a dual one of *eros* set over against *agape*. The epistemological structure is also dual: "repression" is set over against "reality." Science "reveals" our true condition, the reality of our situation. Unfortunately, science cannot give us a positive way of balancing the paradox it discloses.

Religion steps in where science leaves off.[129] Religion gives the possibility of meaning in a "beyond," or a "god." Religion is similar to science in that it also reveals our ontological paradox. Yet religion gives us the possibility of being at peace with that paradox. The meaning that religion offers fulfils the formal requirement for meaning laid down by science.

While Becker thought that his writings "merged" a scientific and a religious perspective, it seems rather that in them science actually drives religion. While his science is modest enough to admit that it describes the need for a religious ultimate, it is not content to remain there. Becker's science is arrogant enough to prescribe the kind of God this will have to be.[130]

A science of humanity, *qua* science, discloses general, structural features of human existence. These features, or aspects of human existence, include things like feeling, thinking, making, buying and selling, and having relationships. Also constitutive to human existence is the need to surrender to something. And this surrender involves the other aspects in some way too. There is little to argue with in Becker's point. In his terms, we need something to "yield" to. And indeed for him it is given that we all yield to something.

Becker is also right when he says that *what* we yield to is important. That is, it is not sufficient simply to set out the fact that we must surrender to something. It does not really matter what it is. Becker tells us that we can either surrender to God, or to a fetish object (or idol). The first is authentic because truly transcendent, the second inauthentic because it is actually a "narrowing down" of the world.

Becker goes on to describe the normative content of this ultimate as abstract, nameless, faceless. It is here that Becker's assertion that science "gives way" to religion becomes dubious. It would be more accurate to say that for Becker science merely opens a space for religion to fill, a space defined by and therefore the property of science.[131]

Applying to Becker's own writings his disclosure of an ultimate dimension to all human cultural products leads to the question: What religious "other" do they disclose? When Becker claims in *The Denial of Death* that science discloses "the empirical facts," and that those empirical facts are final and absolute, he must (in order to be consistent) say that even whatever one takes to be God is legitimized (for him) in terms of whether or not it supports science's vision of "the facts." It has already been observed that the "bar" of legitimation that Becker appeals to is science, and that all religions and cultures are to be judged in terms of whether they are "empirically true." And what is "empirical truth?" Nothing other than the paradox of existence, as Becker has put it! This circularity is significant in that it is not self-aware. Or to put it in Becker's favourite expression: it is not self-critical.

"Repression of Reality" and "Relative Unrepression"

Becker has asserted that all our ways of making sense of life are repressions of "reality." This is constitutive of human existence such that the only way humans can live in a world of paradox is to lie about it—and about themselves. At the same time, Becker says that illusions are acceptable to a point, ... the point at which they lie about human nature.[132]

While Becker criticizes those who herald "the unrepressed life," he seems unable to make up his mind about whether his own "sober scientific," "rounded" and "realistic" view is not also a view from the perspective of unrepression.[133] Neither can he give any concrete difference between "bad illusions" (including Rousseau's and, by extension his earlier one) which "lie" about human nature,[134] and those "good illusions" which "let the most amount of reality in."

And so human existence displays, simultaneously, a universal need for repression and yet the possibility of seeing the world "in a state of relative unrepression." How does Becker know that his "empirical truth" is not just another repression? He "knows" because for him science is acting as a judge, as a "supernorm" that relativizes all other norms to it. Science is not subject to repression.

Does Becker's "scientific" reduction of all cultural expressions (*qua* cultural expressions) to "repressions" of reality not actually fulfil his own prophecy of an absolutism standing over against all others and feeding off them? Is this "sober science" or an insidious kind of cultural imperialism? For of all the cultures that have existed in history only one has legitimized itself with terms like "empirical," "scientific" and "critical"—the one currently facing its own demise.

Becker's is an illusory universality in which repression dominates as a way of speaking out of the modern experience of a loss of control.[135] The modern experience, voiced by Becker, is a simple cry: "We've been deceived!" Thus the conclusion that Becker's qualification of the activity of world construction with a word like "repression" (or "lie") makes sense only in terms of his whole corpus. Since the illusions of control and autonomy constitute the "paradise" that we have been ejected from, life becomes an impossible burden for Becker the modern man.

If however it is asserted that control and autonomy were never ours, nor should they have been; if we go a step further and say that control and autonomy are actually misdirected and unhuman; if we go even further and say that control and autonomy actually promote the kind of alienation that gives Becker his starting point, then we can say that those ideals of the Enlightenment actually must be let go if we are to recover "belonging"—not to some "beyond," nor to some abstract "ground," nor simply to God, but to the world.

Becker's Inaccessible God

Becker's is a cruel medicine. He does tell us that there is "cosmic purpose" and "meaning out there," but in the same breath he takes it away. "Renounce! renounce!" is what Becker shouts at all certitude. If anyone ever were to "find meaning," they would have to renounce it, or else it would become another fetish. If anyone were to ever "find God," they would have to renounce God too.

Again, it is not insignificant that Becker ends with God, rather than begins with God. This is primarily because for Becker the real (which is disclosed by science) must point to the ideal, the creature to the transcendent. But for Becker this "transcendent" is powerful as an object of trust precisely because it is so unreal. And not only unreal, but unattainable. And not only unattainable, but as we shall see in the conclusion to this work, absent from modern vision.

Notes

1. While it is difficult to tie "late Becker" down to a specific set of works, the line between his earlier and later work might be drawn with *The Birth and Death of Meaning*, 2nd. ed. (New York: Free Press, 1971). It should be noted that while the material dates from Berkeley in 1966, *The Lost Science of Man* contains an introduction, written some four years later, which has the flavour of the later Becker:

> The best we can hope for is to avoid the death and decay of mankind by using the feeble light of reason and the ideal of betterment. This reason and this ideal then becomes a way of transacting dialectically with a fundamentally irrational and evil world; they help to hold that world somewhat in balance, to "save it from itself" and its own inherent forces of destruction. *The Lost Science of Man* (New York: George Braziller, 1971), xi.

2. Sam Keen, interview, "The Heroics of Everyday Life: A Theorist of Death Confronts His Own End," *Psychology Today*, April 1974: 74.

3. Keen, "Heroics": 80.

4. *Escape from Evil* (New York: Free Press, 1975), xviii.

5. *Birth and Death*, 2nd ed., ix.

6. *Escape*, xviii.

7. Keen, "Heroics": 74.

8. *Birth and Death*, 2nd ed., ix.

9. *Escape*, xviii

10. Becker's provisional title for *The Denial of Death* (New York: Free Press, 1973), was *The Natural Merger of Science and Tragedy*. Harvey Bates, "Letters from Ernest," *The Christian Century* 94:8 (9 March, 1977): 227. Becker subtitled the chapter on the development of the ego in *Birth and Death*, 2nd ed., "Introduction to the *Birth of Tragedy*."

11. Keen, "Heroics": 74.

12. *Denial*, xi.

13. *Denial*, 281.

14. *Denial*, 282.

15. The three sections in *The Denial of Death* are as follows: I. The Depth Psychology of Heroism; II. The Failures of Heroism; III. The Dilemmas of Heroism.

16. *Denial*, x.

17. *Denial*, 1.

18. Becker cites Nietzsche's "will to power" as an expression of the heroic urge. William James's idea of the earth as a theatre for human heroism is also a philosophical expression of the hero idea.

19. See especially Becker's reinterpretation of the thought of Soren Kierkegaard. Becker notes that all religions feature a hero that has risen from the dead.

20. On the theme of "encyclopedia" in modernity, see Mark C. Taylor, *Erring: A Postmodern A/Theology* (Chicago: University of Chicago Press, 1984), 76f.

21. By the seductive power of the symbol, Becker did not mean to invalidate symbolic existence. This is the way humans have adapted to nature. Rather, Becker meant a deception wherein we come to see our life problems confined within a symbolic universe, thus cutting us off from the world. So he writes that,

> *Man's playforms may even outwit human adaptation itself.* The fiction can become greater than physical reality; the struggle for survival becomes a struggle with the ideas one has inherited, and not with Nature itself. *Beyond Alienation*, 141.

22. *Denial*, 15. In 13-20 Becker puts the two options in terms of a "nurture" vs. "nature" or a "healthy minded" vs. "morbidly minded" perspective on human ills. While he does not explicitly mention his own views in this context, it is clear that Becker himself moved from the former to the latter perspective in his own appraisal of human existence.

23. *Birth and Death*, 2nd ed., 77.

24. *Denial*, 2.

25. As in *Denial*, 2-3.

26. ix.

27. 13.

28. *The Structure of Evil* (New York: George Braziller, 1968), ch. 12.
29. See *Denial*, 13-14.
30. *Denial*, 19
31. *Denial*, 18.
32. *Escape*, 4.
33. *Denial*, 16. Becker gets the metaphor of the skull from William James's *The Varieties of Religious Experience*, 1902 (New York: Mentor Books, 1958), 251. The phrase "New Athenian Celebration of Man" comes from *Structure*, 221.
34. 38.
35. *Denial*, 36.
36. *Denial*, 36-37
37. *Denial*, 39.
38. *Denial*, 40.
39. And, of course, in primary narcissism, repression and fear of death.
40. The theme of Becker's conflation of finitude and creatureliness will be examined in detail below.
41. *Birth and Death*, 2nd. ed., 196.
42. *Denial*, 26.
43. On the distinction between monism and dualism that has informed this exposition, see James H. Olthuis's "Models of Humankind in Theology and Psychology," unpublished paper, Institute for Christian Studies, 1989, 24-28. An excerpt from this paper may clarify the present use of the terms:

> The drive of a monism is to actualize ... unity in the diversity of common human experiences.... The goal of life is to supercede the divergent dimensions and to be integrated or in tune with the underlying, pervasive and original oneness. Monisms seek to realize the unity that is.... The drive of dualism is to acheive a measure of cooperation and integration between disparate elements; ... the goal of life is to take the lower reality into as viable a union with the higher reality as possible.... Dualism seeks to forge a unity that never was (27).

44. *Escape*, 1.
45. *Birth and Death*, 2nd ed., 80.
46. Eugene Bianchi in "Death and Transcendence in Ernest Becker," *Religion in Life* 46 (1977), 460f. and Lucy Bregman, "Three Psycho-Mythologies of Death: Becker, Hillman and Lifton," *Journal of the American Academy of Religion* LII: 3 (1983): 461f., both make this allegation. Likewise in an otherwise appreciative review of *Escape from Evil*, Robert Jay Lifton expresses his main reservation as being Becker's "Cartesianism," *New York Times Book Review* (12 Dec. 1975): 4. Bianchi portrays Becker's dualism as resembling a Manichean dualism, while Bregman sees Becker in a more traditional, Cartesian dualism. Sally Kenel claims, to the contrary,

that both of these categorizations are impositions onto the theory of Becker, which she calls "dialectical."

It seems, however, that Becker actually moves *from* a dialectical theory (in which a single principle of striving interprets human existence) *to* a dualistic theory in which two contrary and irreconcilable motives interpret human existence. While it is granted that Becker's theory is neither a simple Cartesianism nor a Manicheanism, the conclusion that therefore the category "dualism" cannot apply need not follow. And so when Kenel points out on 109 of her *Mortal Gods* that "A strictly dualistic interpretation of Becker's thought would advocate the choice of immortality over mortality ... ," I would disagree. Manicheanism and Cartesianism are not the only kinds of dualistic models of humankind.

Becker's dualism resembles most closely that of Soren Kierkegaard, with whom he develops his discussion of "individuality in finitude" in *Denial*, 92. Kierkegaard presents the person as a union of finitude (the lack of infinitude) and infinitude (the lack of finitude), of necessity and possibility. Both finitude and infinitude have their own character, and their own despair. "Finitude's despair is the lack of possibility" and "infinitude's despair is the lack of necessity." See *The Sickness Unto Death*, translated and introduced by Howard V. Hong and Edna H. Hong (Princeton, NJ: Princeton University Press, 1980), 30-37. Kierkegaard's solution is not to set one over against the other, but to assert the self in relation to God, which serves to balance the duality of finitude and infinitude. Later in this chapter Becker's struggle toward a similar balance will become apparent.

47. More specifically, Becker's dualism may be named "geneticistic dualism." The term is used by D.H.Th. Vollenhoven in his problem-historical approach to the history of philosophy. For uses of that approach see Arnold de Graaf, "Towards a New Anthropological Model," in *Hearing and Doing: Philosophical Essays Dedication to H. Evan Runner* (Toronto: Wedge, 1989), 97-118; Calvin G. Seerveld, "Biblical Wisdom Underneath Vollenhoven's Categories for Philosophical Historiography," *Philosophia Reformata* 38 (1973): 127-43; Olthuis, "Models."

48. Becker discusses these motives on 150-55 of *Denial of Death*.

49. *Denial*, 152-53.

50. This may sound very "redemptive" in the Christian sense of selfless sacrifice out of a sense of love for the other, as for example when Christ "laid down his life for his friends." But Becker does not have this in mind. Laying down one's life is not a free act of a self; but rather a necessary part of what constitutes humanness.

51. *Denial*, 151-53.

52. *Denial*, 155.

53. *Escape*, 34-35.

54. Cf. *Beyond Alienation*, 259.

55. Although Becker *does* relate them. Projecting guilt onto an act (such as masturbation) is much easier to deal with than the guilt of being a creature with a penis.
56. *Escape*, 136.
57. *Escape*, 36.
58. *Denial*, 26.
59. Volney Gay, "Winnecott's Contribution to Religious Studies: The Resurrection of the Culture Hero," *Journal of the American Academy of Religion* LI: 3 (1983): 373.
60. *Denial*, 58.
61. *Denial*, 69.
62. *Denial*, 69.
63. Gay, "Hero": 373. It is interesting to note that Prometheus blinded humans to their own death.
64. *Denial*, 142.
65. *Denial*, 143.
66. *Denial*, 143, 148. We "participate" in the immortality of the other. Hence the transference dynamic refers especially to the "yielding" or *agape* motive.
67. *Denial*, 156.
68. *Denial*, 147.
69. *Denial*, 156. Again note the implicit idea of "cultural man" as automaton.
70. *Denial*, 157.
71. One of the most profound—and sadistic—statements of Becker's point here (and those points that follow) is found in the musical "The Wall" by Pink Floyd (CBS XP2T-36183). In it a young boy (reputed to be Floyd's own Roger Watters) loses his father in the second world war and is raised by his mother. Protected from the "evil" world, he builds a wall around himself, brick by brick. Every setback, every punishment, every threat is "another brick in the wall." Eventually the character, pumped up by drugs, finds himself completely enclosed, asking, "Is there anybody out there?" Simultaneously, those on the "outside" are asking, "Is there anybody in there?" As he becomes "comfortably numb," the character's defensiveness becomes projected against all outsiders (which he names "coons," "Jews," and "those with spots") and he becomes (whether in a drug induced hallucination or in "reality"—we are not told) a neo-Nazi idol. Judged by the hypocritical society that had sent his father off to the war to die in the first place, by his mother, and by his "peers," he is sentenced to be "exposed." The album draws to a close with the judge and the rest of the cast crying "tear down the wall!"

This work is "profound" because it expresses the same mood in late modernity found in Becker, the same despair. It is "sadistic" because it "tears down" but fails to build up.
72. Society wants to be the one to decide how people are to transcend death; it will tolerate the *causa sui* project only if it fits into the standard social project. Otherwise

there is the alarm of "Anarchy!" People fear that the standard morality will be undermined—another way of saying that they fear they will no longer be able to control life and death. *Denial*, 46.

73. The concept "character armour" is derived from Wilhelm Reich. Becker used it for the first time in his exposition of the film "The Pawnbroker" in *Angel in Armor*. "Character armor ... refers literally to the arming of the personality so that it can manoeuvre in a threatening world." *Angel in Armor* (New York: Braziller, 1969), 83. This essay is dated "August 1967."

74. Letter to Harvey Bates dated April 8, 1969, in "Letters": 225.

75. See *Denial*, 53-64.

76. As a clarification it should be noted that surrender for Becker is a *denial* if it takes place within culture. Later the way Becker deals with cultures as religions shall be noted.

77. Becker's theory is also guilty here. It also is a quest for an absolute that will relativize all others to it. In Becker's case, as shall become apparent, that absolute is embodied in "religion" which judges all cultures from a "transcendent" point of view.

78. Becker did most of his writing during the US war in Vietnam, where on a daily basis Americans were exposed to atrocities committed by both sides. Becker's references to this war demonstrate that he grieved much over it. See for example *Escape*, 98, 99, 106, 108, 117.

79. *Escape*, 113.

80. For illustrations of this, see Sam Keen's book *Faces of the Enemy: Reflections of the Hostile Imagination* (San Francisco: Harper Collins, 1991), 113-16. Keen's whole book is worth reading for its illustrations of Becker's ideas, especially 64-65 ("The enemy as death").

81. One hardly needs to mention the horror of "ethnic cleansing" revealed most recently in Bosnia. See Maggie O'Kane, "The Horrors, Fears and Tears of Ethnic Cleansing," *Manchester Guardian Weekly*, August 9, 1992: 1.

82. Keen, "Heroics": 72.

83. Scapegoating is the creation of a focus for our life-denying energies.

84. See Jessica Benjamin's *The Bonds of Love* (New York: Pantheon Books, 1987), chapter 2.

85. *The National Interest* (Summer 1989): 3-18.

86. This is something which both US presidential candidates in the 1992 election tried to credit to America. Even Bill Clinton claimed in his acceptance speech at the Democratic National Convention that "we" won the cold war, completely ignoring the internal dynamics of Soviet politics and the spirit of the Soviet people. George Bush's agreement with this position and his ongoing attempt to create Saddam

Hussein as the new enemy are also notable. In the meantime, women in the new, "liberated" Kuwait still are not allowed to vote.

87. Jean Francois Lyotard has defined the postmodern condition as "incredulity toward metanarratives," issuing forth in a legitimation crisis. "The Post Modern Condition" in *After Philosophy*, Kenneth Baynes, James Bohman and Thomas MacCarthy, eds. (Cambridge, MA: MIT Press, 1987), 67-94.

88. See the introduction to Becker's *Angel in Armor* (Free Press, 1969).

89. 7.

90. 7.

91. Otto Rank, cited in *Denial*, 62. Note the shift from "man is good but society renders him evil."

92. *Escape*, xviii.

93. *Escape*, 124.

94. The careful reader will have noticed that the generic human "we" has now slid into the "we" of "we moderns."

95. Douglas John Hall has described Becker's theory this way in his *Thinking the Faith* (Minneapolis: Augsburg, 1990), 177-89.

96. *Birth and Death*, 2nd ed., 159.

97. See *Denial*, chapter six

98. See especially ch. 3 of *Denial of Death*.

99. See Norman O. Brown's *Life Against Death* (Middletown: Wesleyan Press, 1959), 307f.

100. *Denial*, 13-20.

101. Becker cites Marcuse's *Eros and Civilization* (New York: Vintage, 1962).

102. *Denial*, 264-65. Becker also notes that the elimination of "death" is an ideal bequeathed by the Enlightenment. The claim that eliminating death would eliminate the fear of death is itself energized by the fear of death. Eliminating the fear of death would mean nothing other than the creation of a new species of animal on the earth. While this work disagrees with the idea that the fear of death is necessary to human existence, Becker has a point in claiming that our creaturely "limits" is something that the Enlightenment could never come to terms with. See his further discussion in *Denial*, 268.

103. *Escape*, 145. It is interesting to note two things in this connection. First, as Charles Taylor has pointed out, it is Enlightenment humans that have burdened themselves with the "universal" relieving of human suffering. *Sources of the Self* (Harvard: 1989). Second, these enemies of "hunger and oppression" are, like many "directional" (normative vs. anti normative) entities in Becker's scheme, abstract rather than concrete. Perhaps this is due to the "universal" thrust of his work, which makes him unwilling to express it in particularities. But this is inconsistent with his own theory. He has argued that we need "concrete" enemies. Telling a population that "we need to end hunger and oppression" remains at too abstract a level to be useful. In fact it could be argued that such talk is useful to politicians in that it supplies good rhetorical resources without tying them to concrete proposals to alleviate "particular" instances of suffering.

104. *Birth and Death*, 2nd ed., 37.

105. *Denial*, 68-69. Becker misses an important aspect of the Genesis story of the fall: that it is God who provides the covering for Adam and Eve. If culture is the way we cover our nakedness in order to disguise our real plight, as Becker asserts, then culture is a covering for weakness.

106. *Birth and Death*, 2nd ed., 178.

107. Keen, "Heroics": 72.

108. *Denial*, 285. The interpolations are added.

109. *Denial*, 6

110. Again we emphasize that Becker rarely defines his terms with precision, probably to mix as much scholarship as he can into each. He does say that culture is "a second world, a world of humanly-created meaning." *Denial*, 189.

111. Becker uses the phrase "balance of cultural illusion and natural reality." *Denial*, 188. This is not the same as "balancing the motives" language, since here culture is "one of the pans" instead of the scales themselves.

112. "Culture is sacred.... Culture is ... supernatural, and all systematizations of culture have in the end the same goal: to raise men above nature...." *Escape*, 4. Note that Becker also says that "The origin of human drivenness is religious because man experiences creatureliness...." *Escape*, 31. See also ibid, 64, 73, 115.

113. "Man transcends death ... by finding a meaning for his life, some kind of larger scheme into which he fits...." *Escape*, 3.

114. Becker says that every society is a "religion" because it is a codified hero system. The reader will recall Becker's connection between religion and the resurrected hero that he thought a universal feature of religion. *Denial*, 7.

115. Parents, social groups and other leaders "represent" the powers of the universe to the members of the society. *Denial*, 152.

116. *Birth and Death*, 2nd ed., 188.

117. *Denial*, 147.

118. *Denial*, 174.

119. See the chapter, "The Theological Dimension," in *Beyond Alienation*.

120. *Denial*, 92.

121. *Birth and Death*, 2nd ed., 190.

122. *Denial*, 166.

123. *Denial*, 166.

124. Becker would say that God's absolute transcendence "reveals" our finitude *via negativa*.

125. In her fine article, "Becker's Anthropology: The Shape of Finitude," *Horizons* 9:1 (1982): 23-36.

126. Kopas, "Becker's Anthropology": 32.

127. If Becker had used the language of "creatureliness," then he might have been helped to see that "creaturely" existence not only reveals that there is a God, but that this God does have character understandable by analogy from creation.

128. It would not be stretching things too far to say that Becker is offering us a thinly veiled salvation by works. He does talk about grace, but only as a *praeporatium evangelicum*. Some people, by accidents of history, find it easier to be self-critical. They are "predisposed" to make self-critical choices. This is tantamount to saying grace equals luck. We are still saved by making a contribution to life.

129. Let's note very carefully that Becker talks about "religion" in a unitary sense, with little discrimination of the differences in "religions."

130. Interestingly Becker says that redemption comes for us not from God, but from a *conceptualization* of God. *Denial*, 168. Cf. also 198 where he claims that it is a world view that cures sin—understood as "neurosis."

131. This is also underlined by the fact that Becker consistently misreads Christianity in terms of a supposed disclosure of the ontological conditions of existence and as an immortality scheme. One instance of this will be noted in the conclusion. Another would be the following: "Christianity took creature consciousness—the thing man most wanted to deny—and made it the very condition for his cosmic heroism." *Denial*, 160. Jane Kopas comments on this statement: "Becker does not note that it was the condition for cosmic heroism because it was first the condition of a self-esteem that did not have to be earned." Kopas, "Becker's Anthropology": 31.

132. *Escape*, 147. It is interesting to note the view Becker specifically refers to in this passage is the Rousseauean one, the same one he himself had once held.

133. Compare the following statements: "[Repression] is the only truth man can know." *Denial*, 265; and "... the lived truth of creation ... in relative unrepression...." Ibid, 282.

134. *Escape*, 147.

135. This is the problem with readings of Becker like Douglas Hall's which fail to read his whole corpus. Hall sees Becker as providing the need for illusions, granting legitimacy to the practice of theology. *Thinking*, 186-87. If Hall could see how far Becker's human had fallen, he could have seen that "illusion" is actually a tragic category.

4. Ernest Becker and Modernity's World Well Lost

Little blue planet, in a big universe
Sometimes it looks blessed
Sometimes it looks cursed
Depends on what you look at
(Obviously)
But even more it depends on the way that you see.

Bruce Cockburn[1]

For many years I felt ... like almost everybody else, that the planet was the stage for the future apotheosis of man. I now feel that something may be happening that is utterly unrelated to our wishes, that may have nothing to do with our apotheosis or our continuing happiness.

Ernest Becker[2]

Inscribing the Modern Condition

This exposition of the writings of Ernest Becker has taken note of the two images of human becoming that he put forth. The first, called *homo poeta*, incarnated the Enlightenment ideal of an open and malleable human nature, capable of becoming anything, expressing the great life force. Words like "freedom" and "autonomy" characterized Becker's descriptions of *homo poeta*.

This image fell in Becker's later works. It could not account for truly vicious human behaviour. Becker's angle of vision changed and *homo poeta* became a tragic and lost figure. Nature no longer waited for humans to free themselves of their uncritical social arrangements but turned an indifferent ear to human activity. Human existence was re-envisioned by Becker as bound up in ontological paradoxes. The most that could be done was to find ways of acting heroically, of living with the paradox. Characterizing this new image—*homo heroica*—were terms like "adaptation to limits" and "impossible paradox."

Ernest Becker's vision, spanning as it does two of the most significant decades since the second world war (the expansionist 1960s and the introspective 1970s), articulates the modern malaise. As "reading" it expresses a cultural ethos. As "vision" it reflects the insight coming from that ethos. It sees humanity on a stage, playing a part (or not playing a part) in some drama. When Becker says that "Something may be happening that is utterly unrelated to our wishes," he indicates that the stage is strange and alien, the script now unknown, the plot uncertain. If not "apotheosis," then what? Becker cannot answer.

Any vision has both descriptive and normative power. It *prescribes* as well as *describes*. While Becker's vision so weights his description with negativity that its prescriptive power is radically diminished, this cannot be the last word. Psychotherapy teaches that negativity is often an outcome of a deeper malaise, of grieving a loss, of expectations denied. Becker's later works disclose the pain of such a loss.

A vision also *inscribes*, it brings a mood, a spirit, to language. And it is Becker's articulated vision that captures the prevailing mood at the end of modernity, the sense of powerlessness in the face of the world. This final section will tie Becker's whole work together under three headings expressing the features of modernity mentioned in the introduction.

A Resume

Nature and the Irrational

As claimed in the introduction to this work, the modern view of nature is characterized as a stage for the emergence of human life, and especially of the model of human existence envisioned by the Enlightenment. While in his earlier works Becker had held the view that the impulsion of life behind nature was a great process of becoming, even of striving toward freedom, in his later works he describes the life force as consuming and essentially irrational.

This shift from a positive to a negative view of natural becoming reflects a similar shift that took place in the nineteenth century. Charles Taylor describes a transmutation of the idea of the creative urge, which itself was founded on the secularization of a Christian notion of meaningful order: "What has changed was the very notion of embodiment. It was no longer the manifestation in the flux of an impersonal Form; but rather understood on the model of the self-realization of a subject, completing and defining itself in the process of self-manifestation."[3] The becoming of the cosmos was seen as reflecting human creative activity. But then later, this notion began to change with the growth of uncertainty in modern life:

> The great current of nature to which we belong is no longer seen as something comprehensible, familiar, closely related to the self, and benign and comes more and more to be seen as vast, unfathomable, alien and amoral....[4]

The heart of the human person comes to be seen as a "Heart of Darkness." Stripped of the veneer of civilization, the "insides" of humanity are no longer considered in terms of an imprisoned "good" self longing for release through creative expression, but rather "an expressivism with the value signs reversed;" a "radical vitiation."

> The source from which all reality flows as expression is poisoned. It is not the source of good, but of insatiable desire, of an imprisonment in evil....[5]

The shift, discernable in the change from the theory of *homo poeta* in *Structure of Evil* to *homo heroica* in *Escape from Evil* is founded on the fall of the idea of an autonomous subject striving to bring self expression to the life process. It is inescapable that the pinnacle of emergent evolution should incarnate the life process. However that process is revealed to and grasped in a vision. While Becker suggested two disparate pictures, they do have a common thread. Both inscribe the fall of an idea of a meaningful order that humanity embodies. *Homo poeta* is, rather, the embodiment of a striving process. While he once was confident that this process was heading toward the apotheosis of humanity, it eventually became a fearful thing for Becker to contemplate. Nature has already called its own motives into question, having dealt us a bad hand. And so, on his death bed, Becker resignedly admits that "we are on the planet to be used up." It is the destructiveness of nature that we embody, its consumptive drive toward meaningless self-perpetuation. "Life cannot go on without the mutual devouring of organisms."[6]

The world remains a theatre in both images. However this is neither the theatre of the glory of God (Calvin), nor is it (any longer) that of the apotheosis of humanity, but of blood and gore, "a bone-crushing, blood-drinking drama."[7] The conflicted ontological drives structuring human existence force the idea of autonomy virtually to drop out of the picture.[8] Ambiguity is "the burden of the angel-beast."[9] "Alas," Becker mourns in *Escape from Evil*, "the fact is that men do not have any autonomy under which to bring things."[10] *Homo poeta* has fallen.

Response to Evil: Protest or Acceptance?

> We kill for money, die for love
> Whatever was God thinking of?[11]

Modernity's idea of progress embraced the view that human destiny was one of control over everything, including what had been called "evil." It is not too much to say that a vision stands or falls based on its way of dealing with evil. And Becker wrote two major works with "evil" in the title. These works are contrastive, however.[12] His earlier work, *The Structure of Evil*, offered the view that evil could be overcome by promoting a new vision of human becoming. Since "man was good" though rendered evil by society, changing society so as to promote individual self-expression would change humanity. This was founded on a "firm faith in man, in his potential for increasingly ethical action,"[13] on the view that "goodness and human nature were potentially synonymous terms; and evil was a complex reflex of the coercion of human powers."[14] Peppered with "we know now" statements, *The Structure of Evil* envisioned evil as amenable to human control.

And yet less than six years later Becker notes, "I wrote a book called *The Structure of Evil*, but I didn't really talk about evil there."[15] What gives? In *Escape from Evil*, the picture of overcoming evil with human powers, that we are beginning to understand how to deal with evil, is replaced with a vision of endings:

> When we throw a wide net over the seething planet we have to admit that there is really nothing anyone can say about the possibilities for man.[16]

Any utopian ideal is discounted where evil would be eliminated. Evil is ontologized—made a necessary part of the structure of things—in the paradox of individuality within finitude.

It is interesting that Becker can say this is something of a triumph for him. Perhaps this is why he can claim on the same page that "Evil itself is now amenable to critical analysis and, conceivably, to the sway of reason." Then, on the next page, Becker says:

> We surely will never be able to do great things on this planet, but we can again throw something solid into the balance of irrationalism.

Perhaps, Becker speculates, we can balance our destructive urge with reason. But this is not the optimism of human possibility, but rather of a flicker of hope that the human race might be able to survive. Science has exposed "human nature," it has held up the mirror to us and exposed our true ugliness. It has given us formulae for expressing the basic dynamic of evil and told us that "the irrational has structure,"[17] but cannot account for evil's overcoming. Becker brings us to the point where we feel "cursed with the curse of these modern times,"[18] yet is unable to empower healing. Science simply tells us that we must accept our impossible paradox as inevitable.

Science is an investigation into the general structures of things. And Becker's "complete scientific formula" for evil[19] is a structural explanation of evil. This kind of explanation of evil leaves us powerless to protest, since it coldly tells us "that's simply the nature of things." Auschwitz "makes sense." Such an explanation leads invariably to an inability to imagine things being otherwise. This leads to an inability to protest even the worst evil, since even the Nazis were victims of the same ontological paradox that entraps us all.[20]

We are also powerless to protest because there is no one to protest to. A God that we could address our complaints to is necessarily absent from Becker's theory (as well as from his "world"). Becker's God is defined so as to preclude implication in the events of the world. If we could blame God, God would no longer be qualified as an adequate transcendental referent—at least as Becker conceives it. How could a guilty God absolve *our* guilt?

It is somewhat ironic that Becker was so fond of reading the psalms that he missed this recurrent theme of protest to God.[21] But perhaps not. After all, the protests of the psalmists were predicated on the confession that the good creation is God's "mess" and the faith that God, nevertheless, is busy in it. On the other hand, an explanation of evil in structural terms amounts to a view of evil as inevitable, and of humans as perpetual victims. Such a view can only lead to a feeling of abandonment.

Abandoned on the Planet

The modern "secular" view of the world sought to replace God in a realm not actively involved (or implicated) in the world. If evil could be overcome, then human beings would have to find a way to do it without the help of God. Becker shared this view in his earlier work, all the while leaving the question of God's existence open. In his later work, Becker claimed that only by turning to a transcendent God—once again a God not actively involved or implicated in the world—could we balance our motives and find some kind of fulfilment.

Christian hope would agree with Becker in one respect: no exercise of human powers can purge evil from the world. His earlier view that envisions *homo poeta* "composing the real" is met by the view that in such composition, evil reasserts itself. Any composition, or in Becker's later language *repression*, of the real is done in the teeth of the human paradox. In our attempts to purge the world of evil, we wind up bringing more evil into the world. This is the human tragedy.

Unlike Becker's view, Christian hope is not devoid of protest.[22] Even the paradigm human life, as Christians view him, experienced the absence of God not as a cause for wistfulness but as a pained cry, "My God, my God, why have you forsaken me?"[23] What underlines the difference between Becker's and the Christian view is that the latter asserts that God answered Jesus' cry by raising him from the dead. And this raising up is, Christians confess, bodily. That is, the resurrection is not into some non-bodily existence "beyond" creation. Creation is vindicated. The hope of the eradication of evil is predicated on a God living and active in creation. It is this that is the basis for hope.

For Becker, there is no answer to Jesus' cry. Or ours. And so when he talks about dialogue with an absent God in the Keen interview[24] or of the difference between reaching out to God and finding God in his article on loneliness,[25] he really doesn't expect an answer. What kind of "meaningful dialogue" could someone have with an "absent" interlocutor?

And so the absence of God means that our place in the cosmos is taken right out of our hands. We are orphaned, motherless, fatherless. Truth is tragedy, set over against any eschatological "false" hope. Becker's last words on this are ponderously melancholic. They bear repeating because they draw a circle around Becker's work from 1962 to 1974. They are the deathbed confession of (a) modern man:

> I feel that there may be an entirely different drama going on in this planet than the one we think we see. For many years I felt ... like almost everybody else, that the planet was the stage for the future apotheosis of man. I now feel that something may be happening that is utterly unrelated to our wishes, that may have nothing to do with our apotheosis or our continuing happiness.[26]

Retrospect: Ernest Israel Becker, 1924-1974.

And so this study of Ernest Becker draws to a close. At the beginning of the last chapter some of Becker's own reasons for the changes in his theory were noticed. He began to read Rank and Brown, and to re-read Freud. He put Rousseau and Dewey on the shelf. He took a less rosy view of human nature. And yet the radical changes in the tenor of Becker's thought from the 1960s to the 1970s remain striking.

Perhaps this simply reflects the changing social and political situation of those times. Becker's change takes place on the other side of 1968, of the Chicago Democratic National Convention, of the assassinations of Robert Kennedy and Martin Luther King, Jr., of the fire bombing of Cambodia, of the eclipse of the "flower generation," the "summer of love" (Becker's last teaching post in the United States was at San Francisco State commencing in 1967), of the planting of a national banner on the moon. Perhaps it reflects the swallowing up of the optimistic sixties by the pessimistic seventies; a time in which Robert Heilbroner's *An Enquiry into the Human Prospect*[27] and Hal Lindsey's *Late Great Planet Earth*[28] topped the bestseller lists; a time in which sages ruminated about humans being seeded here 20,000 years ago by aliens, and left to fend for themselves.[29]

Or perhaps the change in tone may be explicable by Becker's own change of geography in 1970. While he began to see humanity as abandoned on the planet, he himself was in exile from American academia.[30] Becker's theories were never taken too seriously by the American academic establishment despite (or perhaps because of) his "cult" following among students at Berkeley in 1966. This image of exile is even more pointed when we consider Becker's 1968 article on the "Babel" of modern scholarship and life, and his self-confessed position of the Jew waiting for God to return.

This idea of existential exile underlies his last written work: an article published in the journal *Humanitas*[31] entitled, "The Spectrum of Loneliness." Claiming loneliness as an ontological reality, its spectrum is thrown over seven areas: developmental, neurotic, maturational, psychotic, social-environmental, historical-political and finally individuational. The latter is perhaps the most profound since it closes the circle on his view of emergent human existence, and of the emergence of the modern world. The loneliness of individuation is that of the fully human person. It is "the fruit of a full life."[32]

The individuated person who has gained selfhood, in Becker's terms "who has found his talents, pushed his ambition to the fullest (and) realized his identity"—in short, who has fulfilled all of Becker's earlier conditions of human becoming—has lost the world. Such a person has " 'achieved himself right out' of the agreed cultural world-picture." The "expectations of life have been betrayed." Renunciation is the only option.[33]

And so the individuated person (and Becker certainly saw himself so)[34] "must now himself question the meaning of life." And this "meaning of life" is not just the meaning of the *individual's* life, but of all life. Becker saw a turn to religion as "logical" for such a person, but again claimed that an individuated person must also renounce a present and available God. The person who has "found himself" outside of culture is left "yearning for an absent God."[35]

Modern humanity is left with this "awareness" which for Becker is "the authentic religious consciousness of our time." Meaning-questioning questions are all that is left; questions such as "what it means to have been created on a planet in the sun, why we seem to have been left here to murder and poison ourselves, to wheel and deal in such idiot frenzy."[36] Meaning-giving answers are gone.

The only thing left to say in conclusion about Becker is that his vision, which he thought would "pull the world integrally together" and replace the defunct vision of the Middle Ages, founded as his vision was on the Enlightenment assertion that "man is good" and that autonomy is destiny, has eroded from within. All he can say, at the conclusion of a career devoted to bringing the twentieth century into the Enlightenment, is that "communities of the abandoned" is "the proper level of social-historical consciousness for modern man."[37] This is a far cry from a New Athenian Celebration of Man.[38]

And so Ernest Israel Becker died in 1974 in a shattered society, in "a world well lost." The fickle academic world—which only upon hearing of his terminal illness finally began to take notice of his work—paid him homage ... and then went on.[39] By the late seventies references to Becker's published works faded from academic journals.

Perhaps an alternative title for this work could be "Ernest Becker: A marginal figure for marginal times." There is no doubt that Becker was a marginal figure, and his last article underscores this. Likewise Becker saw humans as marginal figures in the life of the universe. But Becker saw something important in this: that the image of humanity offered by the modern world was impossible to hold forth, and that to hold onto an image of humanity as controller results in such marginalization.

Is there a relationship between "margin" and "threshold?" Is there a way that we can say that the experience of marginalization can also be a threshold of something new? Becker was never able to see beyond the modern pictures he painted, and to his dying day he still talked as if some kind of control over the material of one's life was possible. So we can say that while Becker "saw the writing on the wall," he was unable to offer a new chapter.

Should we grieve over the death of modern humanity, over the decomposition of modernity?[40] Yes we should, or else a newer and better world will never come. The modern worldview must be succeeded, but before it does we must grieve its loss. There are two dangers that may come from not undergoing this process of grieving which Becker has led us to.

The first danger arises directly from Becker's writing. It is the idea that we disguise our own powerlessness by frenetic activity. Becker leads us to the question: are we covering over our stinking corpse in frenzied activity, in buying and selling, of getting and spending, and yes, of research and writing? Were the materialistic 1980s—the "idiot frenzy" of capitalist greed—nothing but a denial of the pessimistic and narcissistic 1970s? Are we Neros fiddling while Rome burns?

Becker suggests a second danger, this time in the Keen interview. It is the idea that "Joy and hope and trust are things one achieves after one has been through forlornness."[41] While the word "achieves" still sounds too modern (set in opposition to "gift") his point is that such things as "joy and hope and trust" do not come "cheap." There is a danger in too quickly moving on to talk of a "postmodern" world, as some have done.[42] Such talk of a postmodern world in an optimistic vein ignores the pain of death the modern world must undergo. This can, ironically, lead to a rendering of a "postmodern world" that is nothing more than a "modern" world in a different guise.

But this work of grieving is also a work of relieving. After all, the burden that the modern worldview placed on people was a back-breaking one. It truly was a command to "make bricks without straw," and is well gone. We can live without the stress of thinking that the life process needs us in order to be fulfilled, that we must always be busy creating meaning, and that we must renounce all socially "given" ways of being (except the Enlightenment one, of course).

But we are not there yet, and will continue to live on the threshold for some time. We still worry about the consequences of the modern experiment: about the overheated economies, the *Exxon Valdez*'s, and the selectiveness of the "New World Order." And it's not even a "given" that we will survive. If we do, survival might testify to a "reality" greater than failed modernity. In the meantime, "joy, hope and trust" must be "in spite of."

A Vigil of Anticipation

The candles are flickering in our vigil for Becker's modern vision. Darkness is about to enclose us, the darkness of death that we have denied for so long. Is there anything we can say about what is to come in the next twenty, fifty or a hundred years? The corpse of modern man will no doubt continue to rot for some time. Perhaps Becker's writings will be an appropriate epitaph.

In the tradition of the church, a vigil serves two purposes. First, it is the grieving of a loss. But second, it is also a waiting—waiting in anticipation of resurrection. Resurrection is not simply the reconstitution of what has been. No conservatism can bring the authentically new. Resurrection is a healing, a reintegration. The final question of this work is: how are we to wait? Are we to wait with resignation, or with hope-full activity?

That all depends on the object of our hope. If we hope in a God who is in covenant partnership with creation, then that waiting is an active waiting. In our liturgy of waiting we signal and celebrate our hope by erecting signposts pointing to the kingdom of the God whose healing we anticipate.[43] Such signposts are formed and impelled not by the spirit of modernity, by a spirit that claims all our human problems are solvable by the application of reason or new programs or whatever, but by a spirit animated by a conviction that the earth is the Lord's—and that that Lord is the one who raises the dead. This is a spirit that dares to hope and sing "in spite of" the decomposition of modernity.

Notes

1. "Child of the Wind,"from the cassette recording, *Nothing But a Burning Light*, Sony Records TNT-77.

2. Sam Keen, "The Heroics of Everyday Life: A Theorist of Death Confronts His Own End," An interview with Ernest Becker, *Psychology Today*, 7:11 (April 1974): 80.

3. *Sources of the Self: The Making of the Modern Identity* (Cambridge, MA: Harvard University Press, 1990), 416.

4. Taylor, *Sources*, 417.

5. Taylor, *Sources*, 442.

6. *Escape from Evil* (New York: Free Press, 1975), 2.

7. *Escape*, 2.

8. This must be qualified because Becker sometimes reasserts the ideals of autonomy and control, in spite of himself. This reinforces the struggle of a modern man coming to terms with the limits of his vision. For examples, see *Escape*, 161 ("autonomy to some extent"), 169, 170.

9. "Burden of the Angel/Beast," from the album *Dart to the Heart*, True North Records TNK 8.

10. *Escape*, 161.

11. Cockburn, "Angel/Beast."

12. See also Ted Peters, *Sin: Radical Evil in Soul and Society* (Grand Rapids: Eerdmans, 1994).

13. *The Structure of Evil* (New York: George Braziller, 1968), 364.

14. *Structure*, 326.

15. "Heroics": 71.

16. *Escape*, 169.

17. That is, the irrational is amenable to human analysis. It even has a kind of logic. When Becker talks about regaining autonomy (against his own pessimism), he does it in terms of such a "logic." *Escape*, 101.

18. Bruce Cockburn, "Gavin's Woodpile," *In the Falling Dark*, True North Records WTNT-26.

19. *Escape*, 91.

20. See *Escape*, 100-14.

21. See the Bates letters, where Becker notes his fondness for the psalms, especially "the psalms of praise to God." These psalms led Becker to believe, even against the activism he passionately presented in his works of that time (1967), that "If we try to live openly and honestly, we must admit that we can do nothing." "Letters from Ernest," *The Christian Century* 94:8 (March 9, 1977): 222.

22. "Joy and hope and trust are things one achieves (N.B.!) after one has been through forlornness." "Heroics": 78. And yet the notion that "At the highest point of faith there is joy because one understands that it is God's world, and since everything is in his hands what right have we to be sad?" (80) excludes protest just the same.

23. Matthew 27:46.

24. Keen, "Heroics" 80.

25. "The Spectrum of Loneliness," *Humanitas* 10 (1974): 245.

26. "Heroics": 80.

27. New York: Norton, 1974.

28. New York: Bantam Books, 1973.

29. In the early 1970s there was a flood of literature defending this thesis, most notably Erich von Danikan's *Chariots of the Gods*.

30. "Did I tell you that I resigned at (San Francisco) State in January.... I have accepted a post at Simon Fraser University in Vancouver.... This makes my exile from American academia 'official,' as it were." Letter from Ernest Becker to Harvey Bates. "Letters": 225.

31. See bibliographic information above.

32. "Loneliness": 244.

33. "Loneliness": 244.

34. See Becker's self-reflections in the Keen interview.

35. "Loneliness": 245.

36. "Loneliness": 246.

37. "Loneliness": 246.

38. This phrase is used in *Structure*, 13, 26, 63, 221.

39. Becker was awarded the Pulitzer Prize in general nonfiction for *The Denial of Death* in 1974.

40. Such a decomposition is celebrated by deconstructionism. In particular, deconstructionist a/theology has sought to revive the absence of God idea. But such work is short on "pathos," celebrating a postmodern autoeroticism. See Mark C. Taylor's *Erring: A Post-modern A/Theology* (Chicago: University of Chicago Press, 1983) and Brian Walsh's critical comments in his review of Taylor's "Deconstructing Theology" in *Christian Scholars' Review* 23:3 (1984). Walsh has tried to deal with the death of modernity in terms of grief. His reflections on "endings" are worth hearing in *Subversive Christianity* (Bristol: Regius Press, 1992), 51-96. The other end of pathos is "poetic imagination." An outstanding treatment of the relation between prophetic criticism, the embrace of pathos and the emergence of the new may be found in Walter Brueggemann's writings, in particular *The Prophetic Imagination* (London: SCM Press, 1978) and most recently *The Bible and Postmodern Imagination: Texts Under Negotiation* (London: SCM Press, 1993).

41. Keen, "Heroics": 78.

42. This seems especially applicable to Walter Truett Anderson's book, *Reality Isn't What it Used to Be* (San Francisco: Harper-Collins, 1990). Two things are worth noting about this book. First is its optimistic spirit. Anderson does not seem to believe in radical evil, and that radical evil can lead to the construction of stories which kill. Indeed the definition of "goodness" (and therefore "evil") is seen in terms of constructing "reality" and in terms of choice (152-56). In this regard Anderson is perilously close to Becker's position (see above, chapter two) that "good" and "evil" are merely terms in which we encase our own society, our own story, as "the right one for all time."

It is interesting to note in connection to Anderson that he saw the sixties as the beginning of postmodernism, "from which there is no turning back," 48. But Anderson seems to replicate *homo poeta* as an ideal: the creative individual, creating reality out of the various fragments found in culture. Anderson's postmodern person, like Becker's *homo poeta*, "finds" its authentic self through such acts of creation.

Again the thesis of the present work bears restatement: that such images must be "let go."

43. One such signpost could be erected in our relationship to the environment, for it is there that modernity has done its worst deeds. In considering the earth as a stage for their future apotheosis, modern people have nearly succeeded in wiping it out.

Bibliography

A. Works by Ernest Becker

1. Books

The Birth and Death of Meaning: A Perspective in Psychiatry and Anthropology. New York: The Free Press of Glencoe, 1962.

The Revolution in Psychiatry: The New Understanding of Man. New York: The Free Press of Glencoe, 1964.

Beyond Alienation: A Philosophy of Education for the Crisis in Democracy. New York: George Braziller, 1967.

The Structure of Evil: An Essay on the Unification of the Science of Man. New York: George Braziller, 1968.

Angel in Armor: A Post-Freudian Perspective on the Nature of Man. New York: George Braziller, 1969.

The Lost Science of Man. New York: George Braziller, 1971.

The Birth and Death of Meaning: An Interdisciplinary Perspective on the Problem of Man. Second Edition. New York: Free Press, 1971.

The Denial of Death. New York: Free Press, 1973.

Escape from Evil. New York: Free Press, 1975.

2. Articles

"Socialization, Command of Performance and Mental Illness." *American Journal of Sociology* 67 (1962): 494-501.

"The Second Great Step in Human Evolution." *The Christian Century* (January 31, 1967): 135-39.

"Toward the Merger of Animal and Human Studies." *Philosophy of the Social Sciences* 4 (1974): 235-54.

"The Spectrum of Loneliness." *Humanitas* 10 (1974): 237-46.

B. Works about Ernest Becker

1. Book Reviews

Bosserman, Philip. Review of *The Structure of Evil* by Ernest Becker. *American Sociological Review* 35 (1970): 121-22.

Clanton, Gordon. Review of *Angel in Armor* by Ernest Becker. *The Christian Century* 86 (1969): 652-53.

Dibble, Vernon K. "Retrospective Review Essay: Ethics, Politics and Holistic Social Science." *American Journal of Sociology* 85 (1980): 1233-88.

Evans, Donald. "Ernest Becker's Denial of Life." *Religious Studies Review* 5:1 (January, 1979): 25-34.

Lifton, Robert J. Review of *Escape from Evil* by Ernest Becker. *New York Times Book Review* (December 12, 1975): 4-5.

Spiro, Milford E. Review of *The Birth and Death of Meaning* by Ernest Becker. *American Anthropologist* 65 (1963): 985-87.

Sontag, Frederick. "The Re-Birth of Meaning: A Human Problem." *Zygon* 18:1 (March, 1983): 83-95.

2. Other

Bates, Harvey. "Letters from Ernest." *Christian Century* 94:8 (March 9, 1977): 217-27.

Jacobs, Harold. "Ernest Becker: A Reconsideration." *Humanity and Society* 5 (1981): 239-45.

Keen, Sam. "The Heroics of Everyday Life: A Theorist of Death Confronts His Own End." *Psychology Today* 7:11 (April 1974): 71-80.

Kenel, Sally A. *Mortal Gods: Ernest Becker and Fundamental Theology.* Lanham, MD: University Press of America, 1988.

Kierkegaard, Soren. *The Sickness Unto Death*, edited and translated with Introduction and notes by Howard V. Hong and Edna H. Hong. Princeton: Princeton University Press, 1980.

Kopas, Jane. "Becker's Anthropology: The Shape of Finitude." *Horizons* 9:1 (1982): 23-36.

Scimecca, Joseph. "Cultural Hero Systems and Religious Beliefs: The Ideal-Real Social Science of Ernest Becker." *Review of Religious Research* 21 (Fall, 1979): 62-70.

C. Other Works

Bellah, R., et al. *Habits of the Heart: Individualism and Committment in American Life.* Berkeley: University of California Press, 1985.

Berger, Peter. *The Sacred Canopy: Elements of a Sociological Theory of Religion.* Garden City: Doubleday, 1967.

_____. *Facing up to Modernity: Excursions in Society, Politics and Religion*. New York: Basic Books, 1977.

Benjamin, Jessica. *The Bonds of Love: Psychoanalysis, Feminism and the Problem of Separation*. New York: Pantheon, 1987.

Brown, Norman O. *Life Against Death: The Psychoanalytic Meaning of History*. Middletown: Wesleyan University Press, 1959.

Buber, Martin. *The Writings of Martin Buber*, selected, edited and introduced by Will Herberg. New York: Meridian, 1956.

DeGraaf, Arnold. "Towards a New Anthropological Model." *Hearing and Doing*, edited by John Kraay and Anthony Tol. Toronto: Wedge, 1979.

Dooyeweerd, Herman. *Roots of Western Culture*, trans. by John Kraay, edited by Mark Vander Vennen and Bernard Zylstra. Toronto: Wedge, 1979.

Gay, Volney "Winnecott's Contribution to Religious Studies: The Resurrection of the Culture Hero." *Journal of the American Academy of Religion* LI: 3 (1983): 371-91.

Geertz, Clifford. "Religion as a Cultural System." *The Interpretation of Cultures: Selected Essays*. New York: Basic Books, 1974, 87-125.

Goudzwaard, Bob. *Capitalism and Progress: A Diagnosis of Western Society*, translated by Josina Van Nuis Zylstra. Grand Rapids: Eerdmans, 1979.

Hall, Douglas John. *Thinking the Faith: Theology in a North American Context*. Minneapolis: Augsburg, 1989.

Keen, Sam. *Faces of the Enemy: Reflections of the Hostile Imagination*. San Francisco: Harper-Collins, 1991.

Keller, Catherine. *From a Broken Web: Separation, Sexism and the Problem of Domination*. Boston: Beacon Press, 1986.

Lyotard, Jean Francois. "The Postmodern Condition." *After Philosophy: End or Transformation?* edited by Kenneth Baynes, James Bohman and Thomas McCarthy. Cambridge, MA: MIT Press, 1987, 73-94.

J. Richard Middleton and Brian J. Walsh. "Dancing in the Dragon's Jaws: Bruce Cockburn's Struggle with Modernity." *The Crucible* 2 (Spring, 1992): 11-18.

_____. *Truth Is Stranger Than It Used To Be*. Downers Grove, IL: InterVarsity Press, 1995.

Newbiggin, Lesslie. *Foolishness to the Greeks*. Grand Rapids: Eerdmans, 1986.

_____. *The Gospel in a Pluralist Society*. Grand Rapids: Eerdmans, 1989.

Olthuis, James H. "On Worldviews." *Stained Glass: Worldviews and Social Science*, edited by Paul A. Marshall, Sander Griffioen and Richard J. Mouw. Lanham: University Press of America, 1989.

_____. "Models of Humankind in Theology and Psychology." Unpublished paper, Institute for Christian Studies, 1990.

Pannenberg, Wolfhart. *What is Man?* translated by Duane A. Priebe. Philadelphia: Fortress Press, 1970.

Progoff, Ira. *The Death and Rebirth of Psychology*. New York: McGraw-Hill, 1956.

Seerveld. Calvin G. "Biblical Wisdom Underneath Vollenhoven's Categories for Philosophical Historiography." *Philosophia Reformata* 38 (1973): 127-43.

Taylor, Charles. *Sources of the Self: The Making of the Modern Identity*. Princeton, NJ: Princeton University Press, 1989.

_____. *The Malaise of Modernity*. Concord, Ontario: House of Anansi, 1991.

Taylor, Mark C. *Erring: A Postmodern A/Theology*. Chicago: University of Chicago Press, 1983.

Walsh, Brian J. *Subversive Christianity*. Bristol: Regius Press, 1991.

_____. *Langdon Gilkey: Theologian for a Culture in Decline*. Lanham: University Press of America, 1991.

_____and J. Richard Middleton. *The Transforming Vision: Shaping a Christian Worldview*. Downers Grove, IL: InterVarsity Press, 1984.

Zylstra, Bernard. "Modernity and the American Empire." *International Reformed Bulletin* 68 (1977): 3-19.

_____. "Daniel Bell's Neo-Conservative Critique of Modernity." *Hearing and Doing,* edited by John Kraay and Anthony Tol. Toronto: Wedge, 1979.

Index